Degrees in
Higher Education

THE LIBRARY OF EDUCATION

A Project of The Center for Applied Research in Education, Inc.

Categories of Coverage

I	II	III
Curriculum and Teaching	Administration, Organization, and Finance	Psychology for Educators

IV	V	VI
History, Philosophy, and Social Foundations	Professional Skills	Educational Institutions

Degrees in

Higher Education

WALTER CROSBY EELLS

42012

The Center for Applied Research in Education, Inc.
New York

Foreword

Academic degrees, as currently conferred by American colleges and universities, vary greatly in number, designation, and abbreviation. They have proliferated along with the introduction of new fields of subject matter, either because those who controlled established degrees were unwilling to have them conferred for achievement in the newer professional and vocational fields, or because leaders in the new fields preferred new degrees. In the field of business administration, for example, some colleges award the Bachelor of Business Administration (B.B.A.) by preference and others do so because the arts and sciences faculties reserve the A.B. and B.Sc. degrees for nonprofessional programs. Still other institutions hold to both the old and the new by using A.B. or B.Sc. followed by a designation of the field.

In themselves, of course, degrees have little or no inherent significance, but as convenient symbols of academic achievement they are utilized increasingly not only by the scholastic world but also by government and industry. Many positions (and the number is growing) are not open to individuals who have not earned certain degrees in accredited or otherwise approved colleges. In other positions, applicants for promotion are distinctly handicapped if they do not possess recognized advanced degrees. These degrees vary so much in recognition and acceptance, however, that a discussion of their development, scope, and current character should be of distinct value to the increasing number of individuals and agencies that have occasion to seek them or to evaluate their significance.

The author has had a lifetime of experience in various phases of higher education and has written extensively on many of them. As Executive Secretary of the American Association of Junior Colleges, he was the author in 1943 of the first volume dealing specifically with the history and status of the associate's degree. Since his formal retirement in 1951, Dr. Eells has increased his scholarly research and writing for national educational organizations and agencies as well as for encyclopedias and professional periodicals in the field of higher education. As a consultant to the United States Office of Education, he has been the chief author of a half dozen extensive bibliographies and other volumes, the latest of which, in collaboration with Harold A. Haswell, is *Academic Degrees*. This volume is primarily a catalog of over 1,600 degrees currently offered by American institutions of higher education, and the 2,600 abbreviations used for them. It also lists 800 other degrees not in current use.

Degrees in Higher Education does not duplicate *Academic Degrees,* which was designed chiefly as a reference work, but supplements it by giving historical perspective and interpretative information concerning the development and use of the principal degrees now current. I commend it for scholarly use by students of American higher education and practical use by those who need to evaluate degrees for personnel purposes.

ERNEST V. HOLLIS

Director, College and University Administration Branch
United States Office of Education

Contents

CHAPTER I

Introductory Considerations   1

Definitions of "Degree"   1
European Background   2
Development in the United States   4
Language of Degrees   5
Number of Degree-Granting Institutions   6
Number of Different Degrees in Use   6
Authority to Grant Degrees   8
Honorary Degrees   10
Privatim *Degrees*   11
Ad Eundem *Degrees*   12
Degrees for Negroes   14

CHAPTER II

The Doctor's Degree: An Introduction   15

Early Nonacademic Doctorates   15
Early Academic Doctorates   17
Classification of Doctorates   18

CHAPTER III

The Doctor's Degree: Research Types   20

Doctor of Philosophy   20
Doctor of Education   28
Other Research Doctorates   37
Doctorates for Women   39
Doctorates for Negroes   43

CHAPTER IV

The Doctor's Degree: Professional Types   45

Medicine   45
Dentistry   50
Veterinary Medicine   51
Pharmacy   51
Other Professional Doctorates   52

CHAPTER V

The Doctor's Degree: Honorary Types   53

Doctorates Before the Revolution   54
*Other Honorary Doctorates in the Eighteenth
Century*   59
Honorary Doctorates Since 1800   62
Ph.D. as an Honorary Degree   64
Honorary Doctorates for Women   70

CHAPTER VI

The Master's Degree   72

Master's Degree in Cursu   73
Master's Degree pro Meritis   76
Other Master's Degrees   78
Number of Master's Degrees Awarded   78
Problems Connected With Master's Degrees   80
Honorary Master's Degrees   81

CHAPTER VII

The Bachelor's Degree   83

Early Baccalaureate Degrees   83

CONTENTS

Later Baccalaureate Degrees 86
Baccalaureate Degrees for Women 89
Total Number of Baccalaureate Degrees 92
Honorary Baccalaureate Degrees 92

CHAPTER VIII

The Associate's Degree

94

Early History in Great Britain 94
Early History in the United States 95
Associate in Arts as a Four-Year Degree 98
Use of Associate's Degree in Later Years 98
Varieties of Associate's Degrees 100

CHAPTER IX

Other Degrees

102

Occupational Designation Degrees 102
Licentiate and Other Degrees 105
Degrees for Women 105
Specialist Degrees 106

CHAPTER X

Needed Improvements in Degrees

107

Number of Different Degrees 108
Abbreviations for Degrees 109
Reporting Degrees Conferred 110
Spurious Degrees 112
Agencies for Improvement 113

Bibliography

114

Index

116

CHAPTER I

Introductory Considerations

> The use of academical degrees, as old as the thirteenth century, is visibly borrowed from the mechanic corporations, in which an apprentice, after serving his time, obtains a testimonial of his skill and a licence to practice his trade and mystery.
>
> Edward Gibbon (1737–94), *Autobiography* [1]

Academic degrees of various types are granted annually to more than a half million men and women by the more than two thousand institutions of higher education now in existence in the United States. These degrees vary greatly in level, in requirements, in nomenclature, in development, in significance, and in inherent value.

At the beginning of this century, for example, fewer than 30,000 degrees were granted annually—less than six percent of the number granted in 1960. In 1887, 60 different degrees were in common use; in 1960 more than 1,600 were reported. [2]

Before discussing in detail the major types of collegiate degrees, consideration should be given to certain preliminary topics which will render a detailed study more intelligible and meaningful. Eleven such topics, therefore, will be discussed in this chapter.

Definitions of "Degree"

The *Oxford English Dictionary* defines a degree as "a stage of proficiency in an art, craft, or course of study; especially an academical rank or distinction conferred by a university or college as a mark of proficiency in scholarship; also (honorary degree) as a recognition of distinction, or a tribute of honor."

Webster's *New International Dictionary* defines it as "a grade or rank to which scholars are admitted by a college or university in

---

[1] Edward Gibbon, *Miscellaneous Works of Edward Gibbon, Esquire, With Memoirs of His Life and Writings Composed by Himself* (Basil: J. J. Tourneisen, 1796), Vol. 1, p. 44.

[2] Walter Crosby Eells and Harold A. Haswell, *Academic Degrees* (Washington, D.C.: U.S. Department of Health, Education, and Welfare: Office of Education, 1960), p. 16.

recognition of their attainments; as the degree of bachelor, master, doctor, etc."

Wooton, in his extensive treatise on degrees, some eighty years ago said: [8]

> A degree is an officially recognized gradus or step in one or more branches of learning; such official recognition being manifested by the bestowal of a title on the person by whom the step has been made. Of the titles bestowed, three are distinguished by their very general use and antiquity. They are the *Bachelorship,* the *Mastership,* and the *Doctorate.* Other titles have been introduced, as that of Graduate and Associate, but these are granted by but comparatively few bodies. A degree may be held to be any title, so styled, conferred by any legally recognized authority, and intended to distinguish it as a mark of attainment on the part of the recipient superior to those required for a diploma.

From these definitions the following facts may be noted: (1) A degree is not distinguished from a title but is simply a special kind of title. (2) It is, however, distinguished from a diploma: a diploma may be, and frequently is, given as written evidence of the award of a degree. (3) Degrees may be of two general types—*earned* and *honorary.* (4) Degrees may properly be conferred only by some legally recognized body.

In addition to earned and honorary degrees, two others have or have had a limited use—*privatim* and *ad eundem* degrees. The associates degree, mentioned by Wooton as "granted by comparatively few bodies," has come into widespread use in the United States since his volume was published. A separate chapter will be devoted to it.

European Background

The use of academic degrees goes back more than eight centuries. The first known records show the doctorate in use at the University of Bologna, Italy, in the middle of the twelfth century. It was also found about the same time—some scholars claim even earlier—at the University of Paris. From these two pioneer European universities the use of the doctorate spread to other continental universities

---

[8] Edwin Wooton, *A Guide to Degrees in Arts, Science, Literature, Law, Music, and Divinity, in the United Kingdom, the Colonies, the Continent, and the United States* (London: L. U. Gill, 1883), p. iii.

as they were organized during and after the Middle Ages. Originally the doctor's ("teacher's," from Latin *docere*, to teach) and master's degrees were used interchangeably, each indicating that the holder was qualified to give instruction to students. Rashdall, the recognized authority on medieval universities, says that the "three titles, Master, Doctor, Professor, were in the Middle Ages absolutely synonymous." [4] Gradually the master's degree became more common in the faculties of arts, while the doctor's degree became more common in the professional faculties of theology, law, and medicine which developed in most of the early European universities.

The bachelor's degree came into use somewhat later and at first indicated not the completion but the initiation of a course of study leading to the doctorate or mastership. Later it came to mean successful completion of one level of study leading to a higher degree. In many continental universities, however, it disappeared, becoming identical with matriculation.

The use of academic degrees spread from the continent to the British universities, where it was developed extensively—especially at the University of Oxford and the University of Cambridge. The proliferation of degrees in the British universities is at present comparable to that in American institutions.[5]

In later centuries, a geographical differentiation developed, particularly in the use of the higher degrees. In the German universities the doctorate became the highest earned degree. In the British universities, however, the bachelor's degree became the first earned degree (at Oxford and Cambridge), followed by the master's degree (granted after a period of residence and payment of prescribed fees). The doctorate was largely an honorary degree, although efforts were made after World War I to establish the Ph.D. as an earned degree, primarily to attract American graduate students.[6]

---

[4] Hastings Rashdall, *The Universities of Europe in the Middle Ages* (Oxford: Clarendon Press, 1895), Vol. I, p. 21.

[5] J. F. Foster, ed., *Commonwealth Universities Yearbook 1959* (London: Association of Universities of the British Commonwealth, 1959), pp. xi–xxiii. This recognized authoritative reference volume for universities of the British Commonwealth is published annually. The 1959 edition lists 633 British degrees then in use.

[6] For a good description of the current system of degrees at the Universities of Oxford and Cambridge, and comparison of British and American degrees, see R. C. Marsh, "The American Graduate Student at Oxford and Cambridge," *AAUP Bulletin,* 41 (Autumn, 1955), 552–88.

Development in the United States

It was quite natural that Harvard College, the majority of whose founders and members of governing boards were graduates of the English University of Cambridge,[7] should follow the British pattern in conferring various types of earned and honorary degrees, chiefly the bachelor's and master's degree. The colleges of William and Mary, Yale, and other institutions established later, also followed this pattern to a considerable extent.

For more than three centuries, the bachelor's degree has maintained the same general significance: it marks the successful conclusion of a four-year course of collegiate instruction, with minor variations. But the significance and usage of the master's degree has varied widely (see Chap. VI). The associate's degree, the latest major member of the American family of college degrees, which was not introduced until the close of the nineteenth century, also had its origin in British practice (see Chap. VIII).

The substantial graduate work which began to be undertaken in American universities came to be marked especially by the earned doctorate. This degree was frankly modeled on the German Doctor of Philosophy degree, not on any British practice.

Further consideration of the history and variations in use, particularly in the United States, of these four major types of degrees, will be found in succeeding chapters devoted more specifically to them.

It has been estimated that the total number of degrees conferred by American institutions is more than 12,500,000. There are probably at least 10,500,000 different individuals who have earned degrees (some have earned two or more) in American institutions of higher education since the first ones were conferred by Harvard in 1642.[8]

---

[7] Of 132 graduates of the Universities of Oxford and Cambridge who emigrated to New England in the period 1620–45, many of whom had significant parts in the founding (in 1636) and early development of Harvard College, 100 were from Cambridge and 35 (including John Harvard) were from Cambridge's Emmanuel College. See Samuel E. Morison, *The Founding of Harvard College* (Cambridge, Mass.: Harvard University Press, 1935), pp. 362–410.

[8] Walter C. Eells, "Total Degrees Conferred by Major American Institutions of Higher Education," *School and Society*, 89 (November 4, 1961), pp. 373–75.

Language of Degrees

During the Middle Ages, Latin was the universal language of scholarship. It was used for university statutes and textbooks as well as for conducting lectures and other university exercises. Therefore the degrees were also conferred in Latin. This practice was carried over, at least in part, into the first colleges founded in the United States. At Harvard, for instance, not only the degrees but the major part of the Commencement program and many college publications were written in Latin. The practice of designating degrees in Latin was retained in American colleges long after other uses of the language in academic affairs were discontinued.[9]

The change in the language of scholarship accounts for some of the anomalies found in existing nomenclature. Although degrees are now almost universally referred to in their English forms, some of the abbreviations commonly used for them reflect the Latin versions. Thus the Bachelor of Arts, the oldest American degree, although more commonly abbreviated as B.A., was for a long time referred to as A.B., from the Latin form, *Artium Baccalaureus*. The more recent Bachelor of Science degree is almost universally represented by B.S.—only a very few institutions use the form S.B., derived from the Latin *Scientiae Baccalaureus*. Similarly M.A. is far more common for Master of Arts than A.M. for *Artium Magister,* and M.S. for Master of Science than S.M. for *Scientiae Magister.*

On the other hand, Doctor of Philosophy is never D.Ph., but always Ph.D. from the Latin form *Philosophiae Doctor*. Similarly M.D. is used for Doctor of Medicine and LL.D. for Doctor of Laws. But Doctor of Music is much more frequently abbreviated as D.Mus., from the English form, rather than Mus.D., from the Latin form, even though this degree is of great antiquity, having been awarded at both the University of Oxford and the University of Cambridge as early as the fifteenth century. The degree of Doctor of Engineering is represented by D.Eng. and, infrequently, by Eng.D. On the other hand, Doctor of Fine Arts is always D.F.A., never F.A.D.

[9] The Triennial Catalogues of Harvard, *Catalogus Senatus Academici . . . in Universitate Harvardiana in Republica Massachusettensi,* listing all graduates and their degrees, bore Latin titles until 1885. Yale continued the practice until 1889: *Catalogus Senatus Academici . . . in Collegio Yalensi in Novi-Portus in Republica Connecticutensi.*

Number of Degree-Granting Institutions

The number of degree-granting institutions in the United States increased very slowly in the seventeenth and eighteenth centuries, then very rapidly in the nineteenth and twentieth centuries. The *Education Directory* of the U.S. Office of Education for 1961–62 lists 2,040 institutions of higher education. Not all these institutions grant degrees, but the great majority of them do. More than 200 offer programs leading to the doctorate; almost 700 award the master's degree; more than 1,400 offer baccalaureate or first professional degrees; almost 600 are junior colleges, most of which confer associate's degrees.

Number of Different Degrees in Use

The number of different degrees conferred during the first century and a half of higher education in America was very small. The earned degrees were chiefly limited to the bachelor of arts, bachelor of law, bachelor of divinity, master of arts, and doctor of medicine; the honorary degrees were principally doctor of laws, doctor of divinity, and doctor of sacred theology. After the middle of the nineteenth century, however, the adoption of the elective system, the differentiation in courses of study, and the founding of many specialized types of institutions led to the development of a much greater variety of degrees. This variety arose partly to meet the need for adaptation to the new conditions, partly because each institution operated independently and paid little attention to the practices of sister institutions.

In 1872 John Eaton, Jr., Commissioner of Education, reported the number of degrees, of fourteen varieties, conferred by each of 298 colleges.[10] In 1877, or earlier, he prepared what was probably the first comprehensive official statement on academic degrees used

---

[10] U. S. Commissioner of Education, *Annual Report*, 1872, pp. 782 ff. Data on earned degrees conferred were first published by the U. S. Office of Education (then Bureau of Education), in 1872. They were continued annually (with one or two breaks) until 1916 in the annual reports of the Commissioner of Education. They were then collected only in alternate years and published in the *Biennial Surveys* from 1917–18 through 1945–46. Since 1948 they have been collected annually in much greater detail and published each year in special *Circulars*.

in American institutions. It was intended primarily for the foreign ambassadors and ministers in Washington who had been making inquiries regarding various aspects of policy and practice in American colleges and universities.[11]

> The usual degrees in course on graduation in this country are as follows: *Collegiate*—Classical, A.B., bachelor of arts; scientific, B.S., bachelor of science. *Professional*—Theology, B.D., bachelor of divinity; medicine, M.D., doctor of medicine; dentistry D.D.S., doctor of dental surgery; pharmacy, PH.G., graduate in pharmacy; law, LL.B., bachelor of laws. The great improvement and extension of scientific and polytechnic instruction during the past 15 years have made it advisable to give degrees in course at graduation in civil engineering (C.E.), agriculture (B.AGR.), mining engineer (M.E.), architecture (B.ARCH.), and other branches.

Thus it may be noted that the Commissioner lists eleven specific degrees as in use prior to 1877. But in 1887, only a decade later, the author of the first published American handbook on degrees wrote: [12]

> I find that most people who are fairly educated do not know what one quarter of the degrees mean. . . . We have now more than sixty degrees in common use. It would seem that a dictionary of degrees must be prepared to explain and define the meanings of all these to the public.

The same author, a decade later, published a dictionary of degrees giving detailed information on 242 degrees and their abbreviations.[13] (These included, however, a few awarded by Canadian and European institutions.) The great proliferation of academic degrees in America, however, is largely a product of the past half century.

Thus in a period of less than seventy-five years, the 60 degrees complained of as excessive in 1887 had been magnified more than twenty-five-fold. It was Thomas Carlyle, the nineteenth century British essayist, who remarked on the peculiar ambition of Amer-

---

11 U. S. Commissioner of Education, *Annual Report*, 1877, pp. cvi–cvii.
12 Flavel Shurtleff Thomas, *University Degrees: What They Mean, What They Indicate, and How to Use Them* (Syracuse, N.Y.: C. W. Bardeen, 1887), p. 3.
13 Flavel Shurtleff Thomas, *Dictionary of University Degrees* (Syracuse, N.Y.: C. W. Bardeen, 1898), 109 pp.

icans "to hobble down to posterity on the crutches of capital letters." [14] How much more pertinent is his picturesque observation today—not only of America but also of Britain!

Authority to Grant Degrees

In the United States, the privately controlled institutions of higher education derive their authority to grant degrees from their formal charters; publicly controlled institutions derive their authority from the legislative enactments creating them. Sometimes these enactments constitute individual charters, but more frequently they are general or special legislation creating or authorizing certain institutions or groups of institutions. Group authorization is common in the case of state teachers colleges (usually first authorized as state normal schools without degree-granting powers) and junior colleges, particularly those under public auspices, many of which were in existence for many years before being authorized to confer associate's degrees.

The early colonial colleges were founded for the most part under royal charters granted by the British sovereign. Institutions in the District of Columbia have been chartered by the Federal Government which has also established a few specialized institutions outside the District, such as the U. S. Military Academy at West Point (1802) and other service academies. These institutions, however, were not given the authority to grant degrees until many years after their establishment. Bachelor of Science degrees were first granted by the U. S. Military Academy and the U. S. Naval Academy in 1933.[15]

The wording of most college and university charters is very general, often giving the institution the right to confer "the usual college degrees": [16]

---

[14] Quoted by George E. Vincent, "The Granting of Honorary Degrees," in Association of American Universities, *Proceedings* (1914), p. 29.

[15] J. B. Sanders, "The Granting of Academic Degrees by Federal Institutions," *Higher Education*, 11 (May, 1955), pp. 130–34.

[16] Edward C. Elliott and Merritt M. Chambers, *Charters and Basic Laws of Selected American Universities and Colleges* (New York: Carnegie Foundation for the Advancement of Teaching, 1934), 640 pp. This volume contains information similar to the brief extracts given here for each of 51 selected American institutions of higher education.

State universities. University of Minnesota (1861): To confer "such degrees and grant such diplomas as are usually conferred and granted by other institutions."

University of Illinois (1867): To confer "such literary and scientific degrees as are usually conferred by universities for similar or equivalent courses of studies, or such as the trustees may deem appropriate."

University of California (1868): To confer "such degrees . . . as are usual in universities, or as they deem appropriate. . . . The degree of bachelor of arts, in usual course, must be conferred upon the graduate of the college of letters."

Privately controlled universities. Princeton University (1746): To confer "any such degrees as are given in any of the Universities or Colleges in the realm of Great Britain."

University of Notre Dame (1842): To confer "such degrees and diplomas in the liberal arts and sciences, and in law and medicine, as are usually conferred and granted in other universities in the United States."

Northwestern University (1851): To confer the "degree of doctor in the learned arts and sciences and *belles-lettres,* and to confer such other academical degrees as are usually conferred by the most learned institutions."

Privately controlled liberal arts colleges. Dartmouth College (1769): To confer "any such degree or degrees to any of the Students of the said College or to any others by them thought worthy thereof as are usually granted in either of the Universities or any other College in our Realm of Great Britain, and that they sign and seal Diplomas or certificates of such Graduations to be kept by the Graduates as perpetual memorials and testimonies thereof."

Oberlin College (1834): To confer "such honors and degrees as are usually conferred in similar institutions."

Smith College (1871): To confer "such honors, degrees, and diplomas as are granted or conferred by any university, college, or seminary of learning in the United States."

Technical institutions. Rensselaer Polytechnic Institute (1824): To confer "the degrees of civil engineer, topographical engineer, bachelor of science, and such other academical honors as they may see fit."

Stevens Institute of Technology: (1870): To confer "the usual degrees appropriate to a school of technology."

Carnegie Institute of Technology (1900): "To confer the degrees in course, and honorary degrees, viz: Bachelor, Master, Doctor, and Professional Degrees, in pure and applied science and the arts."

It is evident therefore that most charters give practically unlimited powers to grant degrees. Only a few institutions—for example, the

University of California, Northwestern University, Rensselaer Polytechnic Institute, and Carnegie Institute of Technology—indicate specific degrees.

Unfortunately, in some states colleges may be organized under the general laws which govern the organization of corporations. In most of these states, grave abuses have arisen. Irresponsible individuals have frequently secured charters, not to found legitimate educational institutions, but to operate "degree mills" for the sale of degrees of no educational value to unsuspecting students at home and abroad.[17]

A few state legislatures have themselves conferred degrees. This is legal, since an agency that has the right to authorize a body created by it to confer degrees, also has the power to confer degrees itself. Medical degrees have been conferred in this manner by the legislatures of Rhode Island and Maryland (see pp. 48, 49).

The power to confer degrees is held and exercised by one State Department of Education, that of New York, which is officially the University of the State of New York, and was granted this power when organized in 1784. It has conferred honorary doctorates for more than a century and supervises rather closely the degree-granting powers of all the colleges in the State, limiting the degrees to a reasonable number (141 in 1960).

Honorary Degrees

Honorary degrees have been conferred by American institutions of higher education since 1692. The number of honorary master's and bachelor's degrees has diminished markedly in recent years but both the number and variety of honorary doctorates have increased significantly. These three different levels of honorary degrees will be considered in greater detail in the later chapters dealing with those separate degrees.

The U. S. Office of Education collected and published statistics of honorary degrees annually from 1875 to 1916, and biennially from 1918 to 1944. Since 1944 such statistics have been available only on a quadrennial basis through the American Council on Edu-

---

[17] For discussion of this unfortunate practice see Robert H. Reid, *American Degree Mills: A Study of Their Operations and of Existing and Potential Ways to Control Them* (Washington, D.C.: American Council on Education, 1959), 99 pp.

cation, which publishes *American Universities and Colleges,* which endeavors to report the number of honorary degrees conferred quadrennially by each regionally-accredited institution. The honorary degrees reported by one or the other of these two agencies for the years 1875–1959 are:

Year	Honorary Degrees
1875	398
1880	372
1890	735
1900	702
1910	679
1920	989
1930	1,347
1940	1,452
1944	1,292
1955	2,246
1959	2,225

Although most institutions severely restrict the number of honorary degrees conferred in any one year, occasions of special significance, such as anniversaries, are sometimes excepted. Thus in 1929, on the occasion of its 175th anniversary, Columbia University conferred 134 honorary degrees, the record for any institution in a single year. Harvard University at its tercentenary in 1936 conferred 62 honorary degrees. Yale University at its 200th anniversary in 1901 conferred nearly 60 honorary degrees.

The five institutions which reported the largest number of honorary degrees conferred since the year of their founding until 1955 were: Yale, 2,644; Dartmouth, 1,907; Princeton, 1,857; Harvard, 1,800; Columbia, 1,525.

Privatim Degrees

A special type of honorary degree is the *privatim* or *ex-officio* degree, which differs somewhat from the ordinary honorary degree. It is limited to the master's degree and although extensively used in European institutions, in the United States it is conferred only by Yale University.

The Yale regulation reads: "The degree of Master of Arts shall be conferred ex-officio, and without public presentation, upon any person who is elected a member of the Corporation or who is a professor in the University and who has not already received the University's Master's or Doctor's degree." (The "Corporation" is the body of nineteen trustees.) The first awards of this type were made in 1900 to seven professors, although several members of the Corporation had been given special M.A. degrees by vote of the Corporation in earlier years. Yale records show that 457 *privatim* degrees have been awarded, 22 of them in 1960. The word "professor" in the regulation applies to full professors only, not to associate or assistant professors. Dr. Reuben A. Holden, Secretary of Yale University, writes as follows concerning this unique Yale practice: [18]

> I have had several queries about our practice in this regard from other institutions, but know of none which has followed it. . . . Our understanding of this custom is that it began at Oxford three centuries ago and is followed at Cambridge and many Spanish and Italian universities. It symbolizes that one has become a full-fledged member of the faculty and is entitled to all the rights and privileges. It is a pleasant custom, sometimes regarded with a bit of humor, but by and large appreciated. For a number of years it was rather underplayed, and the diplomas, along with a letter from the Secretary, were sent through the mail. In recent years, however, a private ceremony has been held in the Corporation Room which permits the President of the University and other officers to indulge in somewhat more formality—and in fact, have the occasion to meet for the first time some of the newly appointed full professors from the outside.

Ad Eundem Degrees

The *ad eundem* degree is thus described by Harvard University: [19]

> By a custom now in disuse, but prevailing during the eighteenth century and the first three decades of the nineteenth, graduates of other colleges, particularly Bachelors and Masters of Arts, were admitted, upon application, to the same degree (*ad eundum gradum*) in Harvard College.

Thus in 1709 Harvard conferred the A.M. degree *ad eundem* on Jared Eliot of the Yale class of 1706 and on many others in later years. In 1702, when Yale conferred the baccalaureate degree on its

---

[18] Reuben A. Holden, in a personal letter, July 28, 1961. Dr. Holden in this letter and in another of August 4, 1961, is the source of most of the information given in this section concerning the practice at Yale University.

[19] Harvard University, *Quinquennial Catalogue of the Officers and Graduates, 1636–1930* (Cambridge, Mass.: Harvard University Press, 1930), p. 1146.

own first graduating class of one man, at the same time conferred Bachelor of Arts degrees *ad eundem* on four Harvard graduates of 1693.[20] How far this pleasant academic reciprocity extended to other pioneer institutions of colonial days is not known. The Harvard quotation above indicates that it ceased there in the early nineteenth century, but Yale did not abandon the practice until 1874.[21]

Master's degrees, *ad eundem,* were awarded three times at Wesleyan University, Connecticut, from 1833 to 1852. The practice was resumed there in 1894 and since then seems to approximate closely the use of *privatim* degrees at Yale. By 1961 the M.A. degree *ad eundem* had been conferred upon 89 individuals. In all cases these were newly appointed full professors who did not already have Wesleyan degrees. Although a few held only master's degrees from other institutions,[22] most of them had already received Ph.D. degrees from leading American or European universities. These degrees were formerly given in private, but in recent years they have been a feature of Commencement exercises. The practice is reported to give general satisfaction at Wesleyan.

It may be noted that in their alumni catalogues, Harvard, Yale, and Wesleyan list their *ad eundem* degrees under the general heading of "Honorary Degrees" although they are not at all honorary degrees in the modern sense of the term. Rather they are a formal recognition that the same degree, presumably of equivalent standing, has been earned in another institution. This form of interuniversity courtesy may thus be thought of as an early form of university ac-

---

[20] Yale University, *Catalogue of the Officers and Graduates of Yale University in New Haven, Connecticut, 1701–1915,* pp. 67, 453.

[21] *Historical Register of Yale University 1701–1937* (New Haven, Conn.: Yale University, 1939), p. 23, reports the following action by the Yale Corporation: "June 24, 1874. Voted, that the granting of *ad eundem* degrees henceforth cease." But John S. Brubacher (Professor of Education at Yale) and Willis Rudy, *Higher Education in Transition: An American History, 1636–1956* (New York: Harper & Brothers, 1958), p. 437, say that Yale awarded the bachelor's degree *ad eundem gradum* as late as 1900.

[22] Frank W. Nicholson, ed., *Alumni Record of Wesleyan University,* Centennial (6th) Edition (Middletown, Conn.: Pelton & King, Inc., 1931), pp. 1106–74; and personal letter from J. W. Spaeth, Jr., Dean of the Faculty, November 18, 1961. Brubacher and Rudy, *op. cit.,* p. 437, following Stephen E. Epler, *Honorary Degrees: A Survey of Their Use and Abuse* (Washington, D.C.: American Council on Public Affairs, 1943), p. 7, say that Wesleyan continued the practice "as late as 1915." Actually it was still in use in 1961. Seven such *ad eundem* degrees were conferred in 1960.

creation. In this sense it appears to have had its origin in British practice.

Thus James Ward (A.B., Harvard, 1645) in October 1648 presented his Harvard diploma to the authorities at the University of Oxford and applied for incorporation *ad eundem gradum* in that university. His request was promptly granted and he was immediately appointed a Fellow of Magdalen College. Many other Harvard men were admitted to *ad eundem* degrees and resultant fellowships at Oxford and Cambridge in the next twenty years.[23]

Degrees for Negroes

Probably the first Negro college graduate in the United States was Edward Jones who received an A.B. degree from Amherst College in 1826. Two weeks later, another Negro, John Brown Russwurm, graduated from Bowdoin College.[24] Although only thirty Negroes are known to have graduated from American colleges before 1860, by 1936 at least 43,821 degrees had been earned by Negroes—37,397 at Negro institutions, principally in the Southern states, and 6,424 (15 percent of the total number) in nonsegregated institutions in Northern states.[25]

Unfortunately, comparable data are not available for later years, but 7,966 degrees were conferred by 75 Negro institutions in 1947–48, and 12,788 by 95 Negro institutions in 1958–59, according to data compiled by the U. S. Office of Education. On the basis of the figures given above it may be estimated that a total of 245,000 degrees have been conferred by institutions prevailingly attended by Negroes in the past century. If the same proportion of fifteen percent of the total number were conferred by Northern institutions in later years, it would indicate that some 15,000 degrees were earned by Negroes in 1958–59; and almost 300,000 for the entire period 1826 to 1961.

---

[23] Samuel E. Morison, *Harvard College in the Seventeenth Century* (Cambridge, Mass.: Harvard University Press, 1936), p. 299.

[24] Hugh Hawkins, "Edward Jones: First American Negro College Graduate?" *School and Society*, 89 (November 4, 1961), pp. 375–80. Most writers on the subject erroneously give this distinction to Russwurm.

[25] Charles S. Johnson, *The Negro College Graduate* (Chapel Hill, N.C.: University of North Carolina Press, 1938), pp. 8–9.

CHAPTER II

The Doctor's Degree:
An Introduction

> I must acquire the absurd title of "Doctor." It will not make me a hair the better, but as times go no man can be counted learned, despite of all which Christ has said, unless he is styled "Magister." If the world is to believe in me, I must put on the lion's skin. I have to fight with monsters, and I must wear the dress of Hercules."
>
> Erasmus (1466–1536) [1]

The doctor's degree represents the most advanced degree conferred by American institutions of higher education. The *Oxford English Dictionary* defines a *doctor* in the academic sense as "one who, in any faculty or branch of learning, has attained to the highest degree conferred by a university." The *Catholic Encyclopedia*—more basically perhaps—says that *doctor* "is the title of an authorized teacher." This simple basic concept of "teacher" agrees with the etymology of the word (see p. 3) and thus, in the academic sense, indicates a man who has acquired sufficient knowledge and wisdom to teach his fellow man some of the knowledge which he has secured. The term itself, however, and the concepts of learning accompanying it antedate by many centuries its use as an academic degree.

Early Nonacademic Doctorates

Certain renowned ecclesiastical scholars and theologians have been designated "Doctors of the Church" by various Popes. The most famous are Ambrose, Augustine, Jerome, and Gregory of the Western Church, and Athanasius, Basil, Chrysostom, and Gregory Nazianzen of the Eastern Church. There are at least thirty such Doctors of the Church; the latest, Lawrence of Brundisi (1559–1619) was designated by Pope John XXIII in 1959.[2] The title

---

[1] As quoted by John W. Dodds, "The Doctor Sees Double," *New Outlook,* 165 (June, 1935), p. 36.

[2] Personal letter from The Reverend Francis J. Weber, Catholic University of America, October 14, 1961.

"Doctor of the Church," however, was conferred posthumously, and involved three requirements: eminent learning, a high degree of sanctity, and proclamation by the Pope through the Congregation of Sacred Rites.

There are even earlier uses of the term "doctor," in the sense of a man of learning or teacher. The New Testament contains at least six instances of the use of the Greek word *didaskolos* [3] (from the verb *didaskein,* to teach) which reappears in the English word *didactic* and in some American degrees which have passed out of use: Doctor of Didactics, Master of Didactics, Bachelor of Didactics, Master of Scientific Didactics, and other variations. The best known of these references, perhaps, is the one concerning the twelve-year-old Jesus who, having wandered away from his parents, was found in the temple "sitting in the midst of the doctors, hearing them and asking them questions." In two cases the Greek word is *nomodidaskolos* translated as "doctor of the law," suggestive of the later use of the doctorate in law at the University of Bologna (see p. 17) and of the modern honorary Doctor of Laws.

Three commonly recognized and widely used versions of the New Testament differ considerably in their translation of *didaskolos.* The Catholic or Douay version, published in 1582, is based on the fourth century Vulgate Latin edition, the work of "Doctor" Jerome. In the Vulgate, the Latin word *doctore* is translated in all six instances as "doctor." In the Protestant King James version of 1611, based chiefly on early Greek manuscripts, the word *didaskolos* is translated in the first three cases as "doctor" and in the last three cases as "teacher." In the Revised Standard version of 1881 (as well as in the New English Revised version of 1961) it is translated in all six cases as "teacher." These variations do serve to emphasize the identity in the minds of earlier scholars of the concepts "doctor" and "teacher."

The very high rank accorded to the "doctor" in the first century is shown most interestingly in Paul's first epistle to the Corinthians. The Douay version translates it: "God indeed hath set some in the church; first apostles, secondly prophets, thirdly doctors, after that miracles; then the graces of healing, helps, governments, kinds of tongues, interpreters of speeches." The Revised Standard version

---

[3] Luke 2:46; Luke 5:17; Acts 5:34; Acts 13:1; I Corinthians 12:28; Ephesians, 4:11.

perhaps better makes the groups after doctors: "then workers of miracles, then healers, administrators, speakers in various kinds of tongues."

The use of the term "doctor," however, may perhaps be traced back at least 1,500 years earlier when Moses, preparing to make his farewell address to the leaders of his people, said (Douay version): "Gather unto me all the ancients of your tribes, and your doctors, and I will speak these words in their hearing." [4] The Hebrew word *shoter,* here translated as "doctor," is translated in the King James and Revised versions as "officers," which is probably closer to the basic meaning of the word. It has no connection with the later Greek word *didaskolos.*[5]

Early Academic Doctorates

The first use of the doctorate as a recognized university title is generally credited to the oldest European university, the University of Bologna. This Italian institution originated in a school of law, founded, according to tradition, in the year 1088. It attained high reputation in the early twelfth century when the famous jurist Irnerius lectured there.[6] Irnerius was succeeded by a distinguished quartet of jurists known as the "Four Doctors"—Martinus, Bulgarus, Hugo, and Jacobus, all of whom died before the year 1180. It is not entirely clear on what basis they secured their titles, but it appears that when they formed a *collegium,* they prescribed the conditions on which others might become recognized members of the teaching body and thus have the right to be designated also as doctors. An early writer on the origin of academic degrees says that degrees at Bologna were first conferred "by authority," soon after the year 1158.[7]

The first doctorates in theology are usually credited to the University of Paris sometime after 1150. In fact, some scholars claim the first use of the doctorate itself occurred in Paris rather than in

---

4 Deuteronomy 31:28; see also 29:10.

5 Personal letter from President Nelson Glueck, Hebrew Union College-Jewish Institute of Religion, Cincinnati, Ohio, November 10, 1961.

6 "Irnerius not only may be said to have created the University of Bologna, but he was the author of a great revolution in jurisprudence of Europe." From Henry Malden, *On the Origin of Universities and Academical Degrees* (London: J. Taylor, 1835), p. 38.

7 *Ibid.,* p. 57.

Bologna, but the best evidence seems to favor the latter.[8] The doctorate was introduced into England at the University of Oxford in the thirteenth century.

In the early fourteenth century at Bologna a candidate for the Doctor of Law degree had to take two examinations—one private and a later public one in the cathedral. The private examination was conducted by the faculty of doctors. There was a regulation that if any doctor in this examination did not treat the candidate *lovingly,* he would be punished by suspension from his functions for a year.[9] Perhaps some candidates for the doctorate in modern American universities would approve of a restoration of this ancient regulation!

In the German universities, particularly in the faculties of arts, the doctorate gradually replaced the earlier title of *Magister* and came to be the only recognized degree for the successful completion of a university course of study in the faculty of arts or, as it was later known, the faculty of philosophy. For a time in German universities "master" and "doctor" were used interchangeably, but the latter gradually prevailed although the diploma frequently read "Doctor of Philosophy and Master of Arts."

The degree of Doctor of Music was awarded at the University of Cambridge in 1463 and at the University of Oxford in 1499, but the doctorate, except as an honorary degree, gradually fell into disuse in England.

Classification of Doctorates

The various doctor's degrees which have developed in the past three centuries in American institutions are shown in Figure 1, which also indicates the number of institutions offering the more common of these degrees in 1960.

There are two major types: earned doctorates (see Chaps. III and IV) and honorary doctorates (see Chap. V). Earned doctorates are further divided into two distinct types—the research degree and the professional or practitioner degree. The distinguishing feature of the research degree is that it normally requires a lengthy scholarly dissertation which is usually designed to constitute a substantial contribution to the existing body of knowledge in its field.

---

[8] For discussion, see *Ibid.,* pp. 33–44.
[9] *Ibid.,* p. 68.

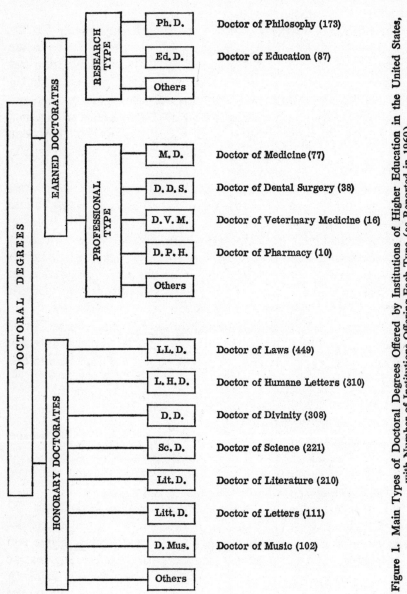

Figure 1. Main Types of Doctoral Degrees Offered by Institutions of Higher Education in the United States, with Number of Institutions Offering Each Type (as Reported in 1960).

CHAPTER III

The Doctor's Degree:
Research Types

The most important of all degrees is the degree of Doctor of Philosophy. . . . General learning, proficiency in a certain part of the whole field of scholarship, ability for teaching subjects in their higher relations, are embodied in the symbol. It represents the most serious endeavor of the higher scholarship in America, as a symbol of research, of training, and of efficiency.

> Charles Franklin Thwing, President,
> Western Reserve University, 1890–1921 [1]

This chapter will deal especially with the two most important earned research doctorates, the Doctor of Philosophy and the Doctor of Education, with briefer consideration of other research types. It will also discuss briefly doctorates for women and for Negroes.

Doctor of Philosophy

Without question, the most important doctorate of the research type in American institutions of higher education is the Doctor of Philosophy. It is now the universally recognized badge of advanced scholarship although it no longer has any implication of "philosophy" in the literal sense. In fact less than two percent of the Ph.D. degrees conferred in 1960 were in the field now known as "philosophy." The American Ph.D. degree, patterned on the German, is so called because the original faculty of liberal arts or faculty of arts (as distinguished from the faculties of law, theology, and medicine) was designated in Germany as the faculty of philosophy. Otherwise the present Ph.D. degree would probably have been called the Doctor of Liberal Arts or Doctor of Arts. (In fact five institutions reported in 1960 that they had recently conferred the Doctor of Arts as an honorary degree.)

In the broader (and original) sense of the term "philosophy,"

---

[1] Charles F. Thwing, *History of Higher Education in America* (New York: Appleton-Century-Crofts, 1906), p. 429.

however, as "love of wisdom," it is entirely appropriate to designate the holder of the most advanced degree as a lover of wisdom, whether that wisdom is achieved in the field of biology, chemistry, English literature, or in any of the other major fields of knowledge. In 1960, the Ph.D. was offered by 173 American graduate schools, chiefly in the universities, but in some other institutions as well.[2]

Development of the Ph.D. in the United States. Although baccalaureate degrees have been conferred in the United States for more than three centuries, the Ph.D. as an American earned degree is only a century old. (It is older, by at least nine years, as an honorary degree (see p. 64). Prior to 1861, young Americans desiring the most advanced training in formal scholarship went to the major European universities—usually German—to secure their Ph.D. degrees. The first of these was Edward Everett (1794–1865) who secured his Ph.D. at the University of Göttingen in 1817.

The Ph.D. was first provided for as an earned research degree in the United States at Yale University in 1860 and was first awarded to three young men in 1861. (At that time it required two years of work beyond the baccalaureate, but the requirement was soon increased to three years, and frequently requires an even longer period.) Surprisingly, however, the proposal for its adoption came not from the general faculty, which had established a special department of graduate study as early as 1847, but from the faculty of the more recently organized Sheffield Scientific School of the University, which was established in 1854. At a meeting of the Yale Corporation held July 24, 1860, a memorial from the faculty of the Scientific School was considered and approved, which read in part as follows: [3]

> The Faculty further request of the Board, that the degree of *Doctor of Philosophy* be instituted and in accordance with the usage of German Universities be conferred on those students who have successfully pursued the above named higher course of scientific study.
> It is also suggested that the same degree of Doctor of Philosophy

[2] See Frederic W. Ness, *A Guide to Graduate Study; Programs Leading to the Ph.D. Degree,* 2nd ed. (Washington, D.C.: American Council on Education, 1960), 457 pp., for extensive data on offerings of each of these institutions in the different fields, and much related significant information.

[3] Russell H. Chittenden, *History of the Sheffield Scientific School of Yale University, 1846–1922* (New Haven, Conn.: Yale University Press, 1928), Vol. 1, pp. 87–88.

may hereafter with propriety and in accordance with the practice of Foreign Universities be conferred for high attainments in Mathematics or Philology or such other branches as may be taught in the Department of philosophy and the Arts.

This degree has acquired a value by long usage which no new degree would possess. Its institution would remove a disadvantage under which our Department of Philosophy & the arts labors in comparison with similar departments of German Universities. The degree which they offer is an inducement which we do not present. Its establishment here would, in the opinion of the Faculty, enable us to retain in this country many young men, and especially students of Science, who now resort to German Universities for advantages of study no greater than we are able to afford.

It is proposed that this degree of Doctor of Philosophy be conferred on Students of the Scientific School on the following conditions: (1) That they shall have pursued their studies for the year next preceding their examination for the Degree in this Institution. (2) That they shall have passed a satisfactory examination in all of the studies of the above named scientific course. (3) That they shall at the time of their examination present a written thesis which shall be approved by the Faculty giving the results of an original chemical or physical investigation.

The conditions established for the new degree—a year of residence, a comprehensive examination, and a dissertation which should be a contribution to knowledge—are essentially the conditions obtaining at the present time.

The author of the history from which this quotation is taken comments: [4]

So was inaugurated a movement in this country, the beginning of a so-called university development, which has spread to the uttermost parts of the land and resulted in the expansion of higher educational training to a degree never even dreamed of sixty years ago.

While thus recommended as a degree by the science faculty, it was immediately adopted as a university degree. The first announcement of it in the Yale University catalogue for 1860–61, read as follows: (p. 64)

It is required of candidates for the Doctor of Philosophy that they shall faithfully devote at least two years to a course of study selected from branches pursued in the Department of Philosophy and the

---

[4] *Idem,* pp. 88–89.

Arts. . . . All persons who have not previously received a degree furnishing evidence of acquisition of the Latin and Greek languages, will be required before presenting themselves for the final examination for the Doctor's degree, to pass a satisfactory examination in these languages, or in other studies (not included in their advanced course) which shall be accepted as an equivalent by the Faculty. The degree of Doctor of Philosophy will be conferred on all members of the Department who, having complied with the conditions above stated, shall pass a satisfactory final examination, and present a thesis giving evidence of high attainment in the branches they have pursued.

In fact, of the three young men who first earned their Ph.D. degrees in 1861, one did his graduate work in the field of languages and later became a distinguished diplomat; another did his principal graduate work in theology and became a minister and author, well-known in America and England; and only the third did his graduate work in science and was professor of physics at Yale from 1872 until his death in 1906.

It may be noted, too, that the announcement quoted above provided for a knowledge of two foreign languages, although very different from the two required of the Ph.D. candidate today.

Thirteen American institutions began to grant the Ph.D. as an earned degree before 1880 and have continued to do so up to the present time (see Table 1). Reports of the U. S. Commissioner of Education for the 1870's also list ten other institutions, principally small liberal arts colleges (some of them no longer in existence), which granted 31 "earned" Ph.D. degrees in the 1870's, when standards for the new degree were not yet well established. Probably a few other institutions did so in the 1860's before the first Commissioner of Education report was published. None of the ten mentioned attempt to confer the degree today, nor have they done so for many years.

Not all of these institutions used the Ph.D. in its early formative stages in the United States in the sense commonly used today. It was not until the close of the nineteenth century that fairly uniform agreement was reached in the academic world as to the significance and requirements for this degree.

Table 1 does not always agree with published dates in recognized reference works. Special effort has been made, therefore, to insure its accuracy.

TABLE 1

AMERICAN INSTITUTIONS OF HIGHER EDUCATION WHICH CONFERRED
THE PH.D. AS AN EARNED DEGREE BEFORE 1880 AND THROUGH 1960.

	Year First Ph.D. Conferred	Number of Ph.D.'s First Year	Number of Ph.D.'s Before 1880	Total Number of Doctorates Before 1960*	Charter Date**
1. Yale University	1861	3	63	5,689	1701
2. New York University	1866	1	5	5,321	1831
3. University of Pennsylvania	1871	10	63	3,734	1755
4. Cornell University	1872	1	4	6,246	1865
5. Harvard University	1873	2a	20	7,813	1636b
6. Syracuse University	1873	1	16	1,129	1870
7. Columbia University	1875	1	17	11,864	1754
8. University of Michigan	1876	2	4	5,230	1817b
9. Boston University	1877	2c	5	1,312	1869
10. Johns Hopkins University	1878	4	10	3,768	1867
11. Ohio State University	1879	1	1	4,814	1870b
12. Stevens Institute of Technology	1879	1	1	7	1870
13. Vanderbilt University	1879	2	2	496	1872
			211	57,423	

* Figures include Ed.D. degrees since 1921 in all except Yale, Ohio State, Stevens, and Vanderbilt; and a few other earned doctorates of special types. Taken from *American Universities and Colleges*, 8th ed. (Washington, D.C.: American Council on Education, 1960), and U.S. Office of Education, Circular No. 636 (1960).

** Or date of legal authorization, without formal charter. Taken from *American Universities and Colleges*, 8th edition, 1960.

a Also one earned Sc.D. in 1873.

b Date of legal authorization, without formal charter.

c Includes first woman to receive an earned Ph.D.

New York University's first Ph.D. degree, for instance, is shown by various authorities as having been conferred in 1887.[5] It seems not to be generally known that New York University's first conferral occurred more than twenty years earlier, only five years after Yale's pioneer awards. An official historian of New York University says: [6]

The three-year scientific course in the college, plus one year in the Chemical Course, continued to earn the B.S. degree. . . . A student who had received an A.B. or B.S. degree (or an M.D. degree

[5] Mary Irwin, *American Universities and Colleges*, 8th ed. (Washington, D.C.: American Council on Education, 1960), p. 1148; and F. W. Ness, *op. cit.*, p. 270, agree on the date 1887.

[6] Theodore F. Jones, *New York University, 1832–1932* (New York: New York University Press, 1933), pp. 83–84.

with a "certificate of literary attainments" from a college), and then pursued successfully two years in Analytical and Practical Chemistry, would receive the degree of Doctor of Philosophy. Thus it came about that Dr. Draper's Chemical School was the first department of New York University specifically to organize graduate instruction leading to a doctor's degree. It should be added that only five Ph.D. degrees were thus conferred, between 1867 and 1872. . . . After 1867, however, Dr. Draper's interest in the School of Analytical and Practical Chemistry seems to have lessened, perhaps because of his growing age, and after 1872 the School disappears from the annual catalogue.

The third institution in Table 1 is the University of Pennsylvania with the surprisingly large initial group of ten Ph.D. degrees in 1871 and 25 more before 1876. While these are properly classified as earned, they were of a distinctly different type from those initiated at Yale and their requirements less demanding than those at New York University. They were conferred only on graduates of the medical school for specialized advanced courses in medicine as well as work in liberal arts following the normal course for the M.D. degree. These courses were less than a year in duration. That they were highly selective, however, is shown by the fact that during the five years 1871–75, while 518 men earned M.D. degrees, less than seven percent of these were able or willing to do the advanced work required for the Ph.D. About 50 more Ph.D. degrees were conferred before 1881. The practice ceased with the establishment of the Graduate School in 1882. The first Ph.D. of the more general type under the regulations of this school was not awarded until 1889.[7]

----

[7] Edwin P. Cheyney, in his *History of the University of Pennsylvania, 1740–1940* (Philadelphia, Pa.: University of Pennsylvania Press, 1940), pp. 272–73, gives the following explanation of this unusual use of the Ph.D. degree: "It impresses a modern reader as anomalous that to graduates of the Auxiliary School of Medicine the degree of Doctor of Philosophy should be given. About a hundred men hold or have held this degree from this School, in addition to their medical degrees. It was conferred between 1876 and 1881. At first those who took the courses auxiliary to medicine received no degrees, but in 1871 the Faculty petitioned the Trustees that one should be granted after the medical degree had been obtained, two full courses pursued, and proper examinations passed. They suggested the Doctor of Philosophy. This was a German degree, practically unknown in America or in England, and there seemed no impropriety in adopting it and adapting it to American uses, especially as this School involved some general culture besides technical courses. . . . In 1876, however, the use of Ph.D. for advanced work by Johns Hopkins University, in imitation of the German degree, called attention to the anomaly, and in November 1879 its use was ordered to be suspended. . . . Those already entered received the old degree."

It may be noted that Harvard University, the oldest American institution of higher education, which has been the pioneer in so many developments in higher education, did not confer its first earned doctorates until 1873. In that year it conferred three: two Ph.D. degrees and one Sc.D.

At Columbia University, Ph.D. degrees from 1875 to 1878 were conferred only on graduates of the School of Mines who had previously secured degrees of Engineer of Mines (E.M.), and who took a single year of advanced work in that field. It was not until 1879 that the first Ph.D. was conferred on a man who had previously received the B.A. degree.

The University of Michigan was the first publicly controlled university to confer the Ph.D. degree, beginning in 1876. The only other state university to do so in this pioneer period was Ohio State, which began in 1879.

Johns Hopkins University, which opened in 1876, is sometimes spoken of as the "first real American university" because of its major emphasis on graduate rather than undergraduate work. From the first, it set up in different departments under distinguished scholars programs of study leading to the Ph.D. degree. It conferred its first doctorates in 1878, only two years after its opening.

Stevens Institute of Technology, New Jersey, conferred its first Ph.D. degree in 1879, and five more in the following decade. The Ph.D. program was discontinued after 1888 and was not resumed until 1955. The first Ph.D. degree under the reestablished program was conferred in 1959, followed by three more in 1960 and 1961. The Institute gave an honorary Ph.D. degree in 1877.[8]

Princeton University just fails of inclusion in Table 1. It conferred its first earned doctorate in 1879, but it was the Sc.D. Its first Ph.D. was conferred in 1880. (It had conferred the Ph.D. degree in 1858, more than twenty years earlier—but as an *honorary* degree.)

Dartmouth College conferred its first Ph.D. in 1885, and four more by 1898, when it abandoned the practice.

The emphasis on graduate work leading to the Ph.D. was greatly stimulated in the next two decades by the organization of Clark

---

[8] Furman, Franklin De Ronde, *Morton Memorial: A History of the Stevens Institute of Technology* (Hoboken, N.J.: Stevens Institute of Technology, 1905), pp. 7–8; and personal letter from Reba M. Clark, Recorded, May 24, 1962.

University in 1888 and the University of Chicago in 1890. Johns Hopkins University alone granted 514 Ph.D. degrees in 20 fields of study before 1900; the University of Chicago granted 141 Ph.D. degrees in 23 fields; and Clark University granted 52 Ph.D. degrees in five fields. In the period from 1873 to 1928 Harvard University granted 1,596 Ph.D. degrees.

Standards for the Ph.D. developed only gradually during the nineteenth century, and many institutions which conferred it as an earned degree lacked the staff and library or laboratory facilities essential for intensive graduate work. In addition to the 13 institutions listed in Table 1, 18 others which now confer Ph.D. degrees began to do so in the 1880's and 17 more in the 1890's, making a total of 47 before 1900. At the same time, however, reports of the U. S. Commissioner of Education show that in 1870–1900 no fewer than 50 other institutions—most of them small liberal arts colleges —conferred more than 600 "earned" doctor of philosophy degrees. In some of them the work for the doctorate was done wholly or in part by correspondence. Some of these smaller institutions are no longer in existence. Others wisely abandoned the practice as standards for the degree became established and recognized in the major universities and throughout the academic world. In Ohio alone ten institutions had conferred no fewer than 182 "earned" doctorates before 1900. None of them attempt to do so today, although all except one are still in existence.

The long struggle of educational leaders to establish the Ph.D. as a recognized earned degree of highest standard involved to a considerable extent use of it by many institutions as also an honorary degree (see Chap. V).

The Commissioner of Education reported that 14 earned Ph.D. degrees were conferred in 1872; 497 doctorates were reported (probably more than 95 percent of them Ph.D. degrees) in 1911, 50 years after the first ones at Yale in 1861. A half century later, the annual production of doctorates had increased to almost 10,000. This figure, however, includes a substantial number (over 1,000) of doctorates other than the Ph.D.

Time needed to secure the Ph.D. degree. The theoretical three-year period between the baccalaureate and the doctorate is far from actual practice. In fact, it may almost be classed as the exception rather than the rule. A study made in 1951 of almost 20,000 scientists who had secured Ph.D. degrees between 1936 and 1948 showed that the median time elapsed between the baccalaureate and doctoral degrees was 6.2 years, with half of the recipients requiring from 5 to 9 years each. Their average age when they received their doctorates was 30.5 years, varying from 19 to 65 years.[9] There is a strong feeling in graduate circles that this interval is too long. The figures given above, however, do not necessarily indicate years of continuous study. Frequently, perhaps in a majority of cases, after a candidate for the doctorate has completed two years of course work in residence and selected a topic for a dissertation—and perhaps begun work on it—he withdraws from fulltime attendance for economic reasons, and works only in summers or at irregular periods toward the completion of his dissertation.

Doctor of Education

The only other earned doctorate of the research type which has secured wide recognition and use by a large number of leading American universities is the Doctor of Education (Ed.D.). In 1960 it was offered by 87 institutions—52 publicly controlled, 35 privately controlled.[10] Several others have announced their intention to offer it, and the total number will probably exceed 100 in the early 1960's.[11]

Credit for the establishment of this relatively new degree belongs to the Harvard University Graduate School of Education which was organized in 1920 and immediately provided for the new doctorate. It conferred its first Ed.D. degrees on a class of five men in 1921, and a total of 77 before 1930.

---

[9] Douglas E. Scates, *et al., The Production of Doctorates in the Sciences, 1936–1948* (Washington, D.C.: American Council on Education, 1951), p. 95.

[10] F. W. Ness, *op. cit.*, pp. 435–38.

[11] Harold E. Moore, John H. Russel, and Donald G. Ferguson, *The Doctorate in Education: Vol. II, the Institutions* (Washington, D.C.: American Association of Colleges for Teacher Education, 1960), pp. 91–92. This monograph lists 20 institutions which were planning to offer the Ed.D. degree, 15 of them before 1965. For information on the history of the Ed.D. degree, see Thomas Everett McPeake, *Development of the Doctor of Education Degree* (doctoral dissertation presented at New York University, 1957); abstract in *Dissertation Abstracts*, 18 (May, 1958), pp. 1711–12. This is a study of 22 universities which had granted the Ed.D. degrees for 20 years or more.

During the next ten years the use of this new degree spread to the following universities: [12]

University	Year	
Harvard University	1921	
University of California	1924	
Indiana University	1927	
Temple University	1928	
Stanford University	1929	
Johns Hopkins University	1930	(Use discontinued in 1951)
University of North Dakota	1930	
University of Texas	1930	
Pennsylvania State University	1931	
Rutgers University	1931	
University of Oklahoma	1931	
University of Southern California	1931	

Columbia University did not confer the Ed.D. degree until the year 1934–35, but has surpassed all other institutions in the number conferred annually, granting no fewer than 308 Ed.D. degrees in 1958–59.

The first Ph.D. in Education appears to have been given by Clark University in 1892.

In 1891, however, some thirty years before the first Ed.D. was conferred, New York University's School of Pedagogy, organized in 1890, conferred on 14 individuals the degree of Doctor of Pedagogy (Ped.D.), which required advanced courses and a dissertation.[13] In the period of 1891–1923, a total of 158 Ped.D. (or Pd.D.) degrees were conferred. In 1922 the University Council approved a change of name to the School of Education, and under a new dean it was given the right to present candidates for the Ph.D. because of the increasing popularity of that degree in university circles. In 1934 it was authorized for the first time to confer also the Ed.D. The Ped.D. is no longer conferred as an earned degree in the

---

[12] Moore, Russel, and Ferguson, *op. cit.*, p. 87, say that Northwestern University conferred its first Ed.D. degree in 1922, but this is an error. The Registrar of Northwestern University, in a personal letter, Feb. 23, 1962, says that the date of its first Ed.D. degree was 1944.

[13] It may be noted that the original plan for the University, which was chartered in 1831, provided for a professorship of the "Philosophy of Education and the Instruction of Teachers with Special Reference to Teachers in Common Schools." This was eight years before the establishment of the first State normal school at Lexington, Massachusetts.

United States, but its use as an honorary degree was reported by 22 institutions in 1960.

In 1958 at least 45 institutions were conferring both the Ed.D. and the Ph.D. in the field of education, and other institutions were planning to offer both degrees in their schools or departments of education.[14] In such cases the emphasis tended to be greater on professional aspects for the Ed.D., on research aspects for the Ph.D. In practice, however, the distinctions between the two degrees is shadowy or nonexistent. In some cases the chief difference seems to be determined by whether a candidate has a reading knowledge of two foreign languages. Holders of the Ed.D. degree are often found doing pure research while those with the Ph.D. degree are teaching or doing administrative work.

Although requirements for the Ed.D. vary considerably, it may be of interest to quote from the official *Register of the Harvard University Graduate School of Education:*

> The programs leading to the Doctor of Education degree are intended as preparation for positions of leadership involving the advancement of knowledge and the formulation of educational policy on both the practical and theoretical levels. The programs are organized to provide flexibility in meeting the interests of candidates with varying amounts of experience and different professional objectives. Each student has an adviser to aid him in developing an appropriate course of study. The course of study is designed to prepare the student to undertake a thesis or project in his area of special competence; such study may involve preparation in foreign languages, mathematics and statistics, or other research tools, although there are no specific requirements in these areas for students. . . .
>
> A thesis or project which provides evidence of the student's scholarly attainments is required of all candidates for the Doctor of Education degree. The thesis may be (a) an experimental investigation; (b) a critical analysis of educational problems, issues or developments; (c) a critical analysis of a field of study; (d) an analytical study of demonstrated effective practice. . . . The thesis or project report must be presented within three years after the oral examination has been passed. While the thesis may be written *in absentia,* those who can do so should plan to remain in residence until it is completed, or at least until it has progressed to a point where its exact nature, scope, and method are clearly established. . . . Before the degree is awarded, the candidate

---

[14] Moore, Russel, and Ferguson, *op. cit.,* pp. 87–9.

must have had at least one year of successful experience in teaching, in an internship planned as part of his program, or in some other appropriate educational service.

Variations from the Harvard practice are numerous and varied. A detailed study of admission requirements made by the American Association of Colleges for Teacher Education (AACTE) in 1960 covers variations in requirements for previous degrees, previous grade-point averages, letters of recommendation, professional experience, age requirements, entrance examinations, and admissions interviews, for 80 institutions.[15]

The greatest differences in requirements for the Ed.D. and the Ph.D. in education are found in the foreign language requirements, but even here the differences are not clear cut. The AACTE study found, on the one hand, that of 54 institutions giving the Ph.D. less than two-thirds required a reading competency, without waiver. Six required such competency in only one language, 14 permitted waiver of one language, usually for courses in statistics, and in two institutions (one the University of Chicago) there was no foreign language requirement unless it was shown to be necessary for a candidate's dissertation research. On the other hand, of 66 institutions awarding the Ed.D., almost three quarters had no language requirement. One, however (University of Texas), required two foreign languages, and 11 others required competency in two languages, but with waivers permitted in some cases. In six institutions competency in a foreign language was dependent upon the need for it in the candidate's program.[16]

Number of Ed.D. degrees conferred. Unfortunately no national agency collects statistics at regular intervals on the number of Ed.D. degrees conferred, but several special studies furnish data which permit reasonably close estimates.

The author of a doctoral dissertation on the doctorate in education states that the number of Ed.D. degrees conferred in 1921–50 was 4,335.[17] Three more recent studies indicate that almost two-thirds of the doctorates in education in the late 1950's were Ed.D. degrees.

---

15 *Ibid.*, pp. 26–34.

16 *Ibid.*, p. 45.

17 Raymond C. Saalbach, "The Doctor of Education Degree," *Journal of Higher Education,* 26 (January, 1955) pp. 37–41. Based on doctoral dissertation presented at the University of Pennsylvania.

The previously mentioned AACTE study based on a 79 percent sample of the 3,256 doctorates in education conferred by 91 institutions in 1956–58, showed 66 percent Ed.D. degrees, 34 percent Ph.D. degrees.[18]

A report by the National Education Association for 1958–59 and 1959–60, based on 89 percent of 18,302 doctorates in all subjects conferred in those two years by 1943 graduate schools, showed that of the doctorates in education, 61 percent were Ed.D. degrees, 39 percent Ph.D. degrees.[19]

A tabulation of the 955 abstracts of dissertations in education which were published during 1960 in *Dissertation Abstracts,* showed that Ed.D. dissertations constituted 64 percent and Ph.D. dissertations 36 percent.

The total number of doctorates in education conferred in 1951–60 (estimated for 1960 as for 1959) was 14,501. If 60 percent of these were Ed.D. degrees (certainly a conservative figure in view of the three earlier independent findings), the number of Ed.D. degrees for the decade would be 8,700. Added to the reported number of 4,335 for the first three decades would give a total of 13,035 from 1921 to 1960. Quite probably the number is larger. Ten percent may be taken as a convenient conservative figure to use in estimating the number of Ed.D. degrees in any national statistics on total number of earned doctorates.

Should the Doctor of Education degree be considered a research degree or a professional degree? Some educators feel that the Ed.D. should be classified as a professional degree like those in medicine or dentistry, rather than as a research degree like the Ph.D. While it is true that the Ed.D. has some of the aspects of a professional degree in its emphasis upon preparation for advanced service in the professional field of education, it is far closer to the Ph.D. than it is to the M.D. or the D.D.S. Ten reasons for the above judgment will be stated.

1. The major distinguishing feature of a research-type degree is the production of a dissertation which is the result of extended research. This is required of all Ph.D. candidates, but not normally

---

[18] Laurence D. Brown and J. Marlowe Slater, *The Doctorate in Education: Vol. I, the Graduates* (Washington, D.C.: AACTE, 1960), pp. 3, 8.

[19] Ray C. Maul, *Teacher Supply and Demand in Universities, Colleges, and Junior Colleges, 1955–60 and 1960–61* (Washington, D.C.: National Education Association, 1961. Research Report, 1961–R12), p. 46.

of candidates for the doctorate in medicine or dentistry. It is required by four-fifths of the institutions which offer the Ed.D. degree, and in the others a "field study" or some other extensive terminal study is required. At least one institution, Cornell University, requires both a dissertation and a field study for the Ed.D. degree. Theoretically the Ph.D. dissertation is always required to be an "original contribution to knowledge," while the Ed.D. does not always have to meet this requirement (see p. 30). The requirement of an "original contribution," however, is variously interpreted in different fields and in different institutions.

In some institutions which grant both degrees in the field of education, an effort is made to allocate major research, such as development of educational theory, to the Ph.D., and applications of such theory in problems of administration, curriculum, or guidance to the Ed.D. In practice, however, it is not easy to draw such a sharp distinction. It would be difficult for any one reading the titles or even the texts of published abstracts of doctorates in the field of education to distinguish Ph.D. from Ed.D. dissertations. For example, consider the following ten cases, all published in the single issue of *Dissertation Abstracts* for June 1961. The reader is invited to distinguish which in his judgment are Ph.D. and which are Ed.D. dissertations. (Correct designations are given on p. 37.)

1. A Historical Analysis of Venezuelan Education with Particular Reference to Progress of Rural Education. (University of Michigan)
2. A Situational Analysis of Public School Enrollment in the Philippines. (University of Michigan)
3. An Investigation of the Expressed Goals of Certain Home Economics Educators and Their Students, with Implications for Home Economics Education. (Cornell University)
4. The Development of an Instrument to Determine Value Patterns of Homemaking Teachers. (Cornell University)
5. An Evaluative Analysis of Mississippi's Program for Financing Public Elementary and Secondary Education. (Florida State University)
6. The Effect of Tax Elasticities on the Financial Support of Education. (University of Illinois)
7. A Study of Graduates of the University of Georgia Who Are Certified to Teach with Respect to Entrance into the Teaching Profession. (University of Georgia)
8. Attitudes of a Selected Group of Elementary School Teachers Toward In-Service Education. (University of Connecticut)

9. An Evaluation of an Experimental Program of Group Guidance in the Junior High School. (University of Texas)
10. Security in Vocational Choice: A Study of Male College Upper-Classmen. (Columbia University)

2. Entrance requirements are similar for candidates for the two degrees: both require a baccalaureate degree, and some require also the master's degree. Many professional schools require neither.

3. Similarities in qualifying and final examinations, in residence requirements, and in the curriculum are quite striking. The 1960 AACTE study concluded that curricular arrangements for the two programs resembled each other far more than they differed.

4. The dissertation for both degrees is normally expected to require at least one year, often more, of the student's time. The finished product has been found to be of about the same average length (200 pages) for each. Most professional schools have no such dissertation requirement, particularly for their initial curriculum leading to the doctorate.

5. The 1960 AACTE study reached the following general conclusions: [20]

> In the main the two degrees, from the point of view of programming procedures, highly resembled each other. . . . In some institutions the degrees were identical for all practical purposes and by the admissions of the respondents. . . . Efforts on the part of some institutions to maintain basic differences between the two degrees while other universities perceive them as practically identical . . . will continue to create a measure of confusion in the profession. . . . The effort to differentiate requirements for the two degrees on the basis that the Ph.D. degree serves research and scholarly purposes and the E.D. degree serves practitioner or professional purposes may never gain wide acceptance. . . . It seems wise to conclude that either degree will best be understood through its institutional association, rather than from any overall aim or national statement of divergent functions.

6. A somewhat similar study made a decade and a half earlier under the auspices of the National Society of College Teachers of Education, based on a detailed analysis of 48 institutions, reached similar conclusions and formulated nine issues involved in the requirements for the two degrees. It found that the chief differences

---

[20] Moore, Russel, and Ferguson, *op. cit.*, p. 78.

were in language requirements, and that similarities in the two degrees outweighed their differences.[21]

7. Sixty-seven major institutions conferred the Ed.D. in 1958; in 39 cases, the degree was administered by the graduate school of the university; in 21 cases, by the school or department of education; and in seven cases, jointly. Thus in more than two-thirds of the institutions the Ed.D. degree was administered, in whole or in part, as a university degree. Normally the M.D. or D.D.S. is administered by the university's medical or dental school.

8. Since 1947–48, when it initiated its policy of collecting annual statistics on earned degrees, the U.S. Office of Education has distinguished only three types of degrees: "(1) bachelors and first professional degrees; (2) second level degrees, masters, except first professional; (3) doctorates (Ph.D., Ed.D., etc.)" [22] Statistics of professional degrees for earlier years have been adjusted to this basis to make historical comparisons more nearly valid. Although this basis of classification of professional degrees is open to question, it is the only one that furnishes comparable statistics on degrees from year to year. It should be noted that the Ed.D. is not here classified as a professional degree. First professional degrees, such as M.D. and D.D.S. are included with baccalaureate degrees. The data thus collected and published in great detail by this official government agency form the basis of the extensive tables of doctorates published quadrennially in *American Universities and Colleges* and are used by many other investigators for a great variety of purposes. It is impossible to distinguish in any Office of Education statistics the number of Ph.D. and Ed.D. or other research doctorates, desirable as this might be. The importance of estimating the number of Ed.D. degrees, and possible methods of doing so, have already been considered. Some writers carelessly use the Office of Education data as if they applied to Ph.D. degrees only, thus implicitly accepting the Ed.D as a research degree.[23]

---

[21] Clifford Woody, *Requirements for the Degree of Doctor of Philosophy and Doctor of Education* (Ann Arbor, Mich.: Ann Arbor Press, 1947), 54 pp.

[22] Unfortunately the Office of Education has not yet collected annual statistics on the Associate's degree (see Chap. VIII).

[23] For example Dr. Hans Rosenhaupt, National Director of the Woodrow Wilson Fellowship Foundation ("The Slow Stirring in Graduate Education," *Saturday Review*, 44, September 16, 1961, pp. 63–5, 79–81), presents a vivid colored graph purporting to show "Ph.D.'s Conferred by U.S. Universities" 1910–60, quoting the U.S. Office of Education as his source. All of his data, of course, are in error,

9. From 1934 to 1955, *Doctoral Dissertations Accepted by American Universities* was compiled annually under the auspices of the Association of Research Libraries and published by the H. W. Wilson Company of New York. This widely used series of reference volumes has attempted to publish complete lists of all doctoral dissertations of the research type accepted by American and Canadian universities. But it has never made any distinction between those which were accepted for the Ph.D. and those which were accepted for the Ed.D. or other research type degrees.

10. *Dissertation Abstracts* (formerly *Microfilm Abstracts*, 1938–51), the most comprehensive and reliable abstracting service for doctoral dissertations, has printed some 30,000 abstracts of doctoral dissertations in all fields of advanced study. Starting with only five cooperating institutions, it lists in its 1961 issues 119 American graduate schools (including all but two or three of the leading ones) which now cooperate in this form of dissertation publication. The publishers estimate that it publishes abstracts of more than two-thirds of the doctoral dissertations produced each year. The significant fact is that abstracts of both Ph.D. and Ed.D. dissertations are published without differentiation as to length, type, content, or quality. Fortunately, however, this publication does indicate the degree conferred in each case, but since the coverage is not complete it cannot be used as a source for ascertaining the number of Ed.D. degrees conferred each year.

Thus it can be seen that in both theoretical and practical matters, the Ph.D. and Ed.D. degrees are treated alike by the major agencies to which one would turn for information concerning them.

Other Doctor of Education Degrees. A few other Ed.D. degrees of more specialized form are offered by a few institutions, including Doctor of Religious Education (eight institutions in 1960), Doctor of Music Education (four), Doctor of Physical Education (four), Doctor of Education in College Teaching in Humanities (one), Doctor of Education in College Teaching in Physical Sciences

---

in later years by at least ten percent, since they include Ed.D. degrees and a variety of other earned degrees. He says that Columbia University "produced 560 Ph.D.'s in 1959." Actually according to the Registrar, Columbia produced only 308 Ph.D. degrees in 1959, but 232 Ed.D. degrees, and 20 other earned doctorates of a half dozen varieties. For corrections and comments see *Saturday Review*, 44 (November 18, 1961), pp. 46–7.

(one), and Doctor of Education in College Teaching in Social Sciences (one).

Other Research Doctorates

At least 60 earned research doctorates, other than the Ph.D. and Ed.D., are currently offered by American institutions of higher education, but most of these are highly specialized and are offered by only one or two institutions.[24] Those offered by more than five but fewer than twenty institutions and their most common abbreviations are:

Degree	Abbreviation
Doctor of Business Administration	D.B.A.
Doctor of Engineering	Eng.D.
Doctor of Juridical Science	S.J.D.
Doctor of Jurisprudence	J.D.
Doctor of Medical Science	Med.Sc.D.
Doctor of Musical Arts	D.M.A.
Doctor of Public Health	D.P.H.
Doctor of Religious Education	D.R.E.
Doctor of Sacred Theology	S.T.D.
Doctor of Science	Sc.D.
Doctor of Social Work	D.S.W.
Doctor of Theology	Th.D.

For a time the Doctor of Science vied with the Doctor of Philosophy as the highest earned research degree, the former for work in the natural sciences, the latter for work in humanities and social sciences. Thus of Harvard's first three earned doctorates, conferred in 1873, two were Ph.D. degrees, one an Sc.D. It is noteworthy that in 1872, when Harvard first announced the new degrees of M.A. (by examination), Ph.D., and Sc.D., one year of graduate work was to be required for the new type of M.A., two years for the Ph.D., and three years for the Sc.D. Thus the Sc.D. apparently was intended to rank higher than the Ph.D. From 1873 to 1890 Harvard conferred 65 Ph.D. degrees and 14 earned Sc.D. degrees. The Sc.D. was

---

24 For complete lists and frequencies of institutions offering them, see Frederic Ness, *op. cit.*, pp. 435–38,; and Walter Crosby Eells and Harold A. Haswell, *Academic Degrees: Earned and Honorary Degrees Conferred by Institutions of Higher Education in the United States* (Washington, D.C.: U.S. Department of Health, Education, and Welfare: Office of Education, 1960), pp. 234–44.

NOTE: Of the dissertations whose titles were given on pp. 32–33, numbers 1, 3, 5, 7, 9 were for Ed.D. degrees; numbers 2, 4, 6, 8, 10 were for Ph.D. degrees.

awarded by Princeton in 1879 (a year before it granted its first Ph.D.), and by Cornell University in 1886.

The strong tendency, however, has been to eliminate the Sc.D. as an earned advanced research degree, substituting the more general Doctor of Philosophy in all fields, even the scientific ones, and using the Sc.D. only as an honorary degree. It was so reported in 1960 by more than 200 institutions as compared with only eight which reported its use as an earned degree. In 1934 the U.S. Office of Education published details regarding its use as an earned degree in 11 institutions.[25] At the Massachusetts Institute of Technology, the Sc.D. is given in all fields in which the Ph.D. is offered.

Thus the simple Doctor of Science degree has been largely replaced by the Doctor of Philosophy degree in all fields, sciences as well as arts. In fact, in the period 1926–59, more than 19,000 Ph.D. degrees were conferred in chemistry, far more than in any other field. And doctorates in the biological and physical sciences constituted more than 55 percent of all doctorates conferred in that period.[26]

Several specialized forms of the Doctor of Science degree are found as earned degrees. These include Doctor of Science in Engineering of Mines, Doctor of Science in Geological Engineering, Doctor of Science in Petroleum Engineering, Doctor of Science in Petroleum Refining Engineering (these two are found in the same institution), Doctor of Science in Hygiene, Doctor of Science in Industrial Medicine, Doctor of Science in Surgery, Doctor of Science in Veterinary Medicine, Doctor of Science in Jurisprudence, and several others. These are usually offered by only one or two institutions.

The Doctor of Engineering also has numerous variations, such as Doctor of Chemical Engineering, Doctor of Civil Engineering, Doctor of Electrical Engineering, Doctor of Engineering Physics, and Doctor of Engineering Science.

The degree of Doctor of Public Health was offered in 1960 by ten institutions as an advanced research degree requiring an M.D., at least two years of further study, and a dissertation. The first or-

---

[25] Walton C. John, *Graduate Study in Universities and Colleges in the United States*, Bulletin 1934, No. 20 (Washington, D.C.: U.S. Department of the Interior: Office of Education, 1935), pp. 201–3.

[26] Mary Irwin, ed., *American Universities and Colleges*, 8th ed. (Washington, D.C.: American Council on Education, 1960), p. 1146.

ganized School of Public Health was established at Yale University in 1915, followed by one at Johns Hopkins University in 1916. The latter institution conferred the first D.P.H. in 1919, while Yale conferred two in 1920. Before the organization of these two schools, according to the U.S. Commissioner of Education,[27] the degree of Doctor of Public Health was offered by the University of Pennsylvania in 1909 and by Harvard University in 1910. It was conferred by Harvard in 1911. The University of Pennsylvania, however, reports not the Doctor of Public Health but the Doctor of Public Hygiene, as conferred in 1912.

Other research doctorates were offered in 1960 by one or two institutions each in such diverse fields as Hebrew literature, modern languages, physics, social sciences, architecture, forestry, librarianship, public administration, and speech. Information concerning nine of these, including requirements and institutions offering them, were published by the U.S. Office of Education in 1935.[28] A list of institutions offering some 35 varieties of earned doctorates, presumably all of the research type, were published by the American Council on Education in 1960.[29] This is the latest and most complete listing of all types of earned doctorates offered by 174 institutions in the United States.

At least 76 institutions in 1960 were offering earned doctorates other than the Ph.D. or Ed.D. Sixteen of these were theological seminaries which give the doctorate in theology, chiefly the Th.D. or S.T.D.

Doctorates for Women

The *Oxford English Dictionary* defines a *doctress* or *doctoress* as a female doctor, a female teacher, a woman of eminent learning, or a woman who has a doctor's degree. The earliest known use of the term *doctresse* was in 1549—"beyng but a younge doctresse." Doctor's degrees were very rarely conferred on women in Europe before the twentieth century, but there were a few noteworthy exceptions.

Novella Andrea, daughter of Giovanni Andrea (1275–1348), professor of Canon Law at the University of Bologna, was so accomplished in law that she regularly lectured to students in her fa-

---

[27] U.S. Commissioner of Education, *Annual Report,* 1913, p. 53.
[28] W. C. John, *op. cit.,* pp. 201–13.
[29] F. W. Ness, *op. cit.,* pp. 234–44.

ther's absence (but was reputed to be so beautiful that she had to lecture from behind a curtain lest her face distract the attention of the students). It is not stated, however, whether she had the title of doctor.[30]

In 1678 the University of Padua conferred the degree of *Doctoresse* on Elena Lucrezia Piscopia Cornaro (1646–84), a learned Italian woman of noble descent. She had mastered six languages as well as mathematics, philosophy, and theology, and was esteemed for her learning throughout Europe.[31]

Dottoressa Laura M. C. Bassi (1711–78) lectured on experimental philosophy and mathematics at the University of Bologna for many years. Bologna is also credited with the services of Signora Clotilda Tambroni, a learned professor of Greek; and of Madonna Manzolina, who lectured on anatomy—"the boldest inroad into the scientific province of the ruder sex." [32]

In 1787 the University of Göttingen conferred the Doctor of Philosophy degree on Dorothea Schlözer, daughter of the renowned Professor August Ludwig von Schlözer. She passed oral examinations in history, astronomy, and chemistry. She so impressed George Bancroft when he was a doctoral student at Göttingen, that he wrote in his diary (October 2, 1818): "Behold, I have seen a wonder! A learned woman, modest, who once might have been handsome; a learned woman, Doctor of Philosophy, Master of Arts, and one of the best informed *men* in the place." [33]

The writer has not been able to determine who was the first American woman to secure a doctorate from a European university. Probably the distinction belongs to Miss M. Carey Thomas (1857–1935) who was president of Bryn Mawr College for almost 30 years. She received her A.B. degree from Cornell University in 1877, and then went to Europe for advanced study at the University of Leipzig. But in spite of the brilliant work she did there, neither Leipzig nor Göttingen (to which she also applied) would consider giving a doctorate to a woman at that time—certainly not to an American woman. She found the Swiss universities more flexible

---

[30] *Encyclopaedia Britannica,* article "Andrea, Giovanni."

[31] *Catholic Encyclopedia* (1908), Vol. IV, p. 373.

[32] Henry Malden, *On the Origin of Universities and Academical Degrees* (London: J. Taylor, 1835), pp. 63–4.

[33] M. A. DeWolfe Howe, *The Life and Letters of George Bancroft* (New York: Charles Scribner's Sons, 1908), Vol. I, p. 44.

and in 1882 received a Ph.D. from the University of Zurich, the second woman to be so honored. At that time the degree at Zurich was given at four levels of proficiency—*rite, cum laude, magna cum laude* (rarely given), and *summa cum laude* (almost never given). In spite of the formidable obstacles of working in a foreign language and under strange conditions, Miss Thomas persevered and was awarded her Ph.D. *summa cum laude.* Her dissertation was "Sir Gawayne and the Green Knight." The university dean told her that "he rarely, if ever, had heard the chief professors speak in such high terms of any thesis." One of her chief professors said her knowledge of philology amazed him, and he "never supposed a woman could show such philological talent." A third said that he knew she deserved a *summa cum laude* but could hardly believe it, since in all his long connection with the University only one *summa* had been given.[34]

The first research doctorate earned by a woman in the United States was the Ph.D. conferred in 1877 by Boston University on Helen Magill, daughter of the second president of Swarthmore College, whose dissertation was on "Greek Drama." She then studied at the University of Cambridge where she took honors in the Classical Tripos in 1881. For ten years she was prominent in educational circles in the United States, and helped to organize the Annex for Women at Princeton University in 1887–88. In 1890 she married Dr. Andrew D. White, first president of Cornell University, and accompanied him to Russia and Germany when he was ambassador to those countries in the next two decades. She organized the American Women's Club of Berlin on a new basis. She died in Maine in 1941 at the age of 91.

The next three women to earn Ph.D.s, all in 1880, were Mary Alice Bennett, University of Pennsylvania, in zoology; May Preston, Cornell University, in philosophy; and Rena A. Michaels, Syracuse University, in history.

The first woman to earn a degree of Doctor of Science was Caroline W. Baldwin (later Mrs. Charles T. Morrison) at Cornell University in 1895. Her dissertation, "A Photographic Study of Arc Spectra," was published in part in the *Physical Review.*

The first earned Ph.D. conferred by a college for women was

[34] Edith Finch, "European Universities and Travel," in *Carey Thomas of Bryn Mawr* (New York: Harper & Brothers, 1947), Chap. V, pp. 90–131.

granted by Smith College in 1882 to Kate Eugenia Morris (later Mrs. Charles Morris Cone). Her dissertation was on "The Electoral College of Germany." Miss Morris was one of the original group of women who founded the Harvard Annex, now Radcliffe College. She did most of her graduate work for the doctorate, 1877–82, under the direction of Harvard professors, but at that time women were not eligible for the doctorate at Harvard.

Yale University in 1892 opened its graduate department to women and conferred the Ph.D. on seven women in 1894 and a total of 36 before the close of the century—more than any other institution in that period. The total at Yale reached 120 by 1920.[35]

The first degrees of Doctor of Pedagogy (Ped.D. or Pd.D.) earned by women were conferred in 1891 by New York University on Emily Ida Conant (her dissertation: "The Relation of Psychology to Pedagogy") and on Harriet E. Hunt (her dissertation: "The Dominant Seventh in Education"). The first Ed.D. earned by a woman was conferred by Harvard University in 1922 on Lorna Myrtle Hodgkinson, whose dissertation, was "A State Program for the Diagnosis and Treatment of Atypical Children in Public School Systems."

From 1877 to 1900 at least 229 doctoral degrees of the research type were conferred on women by 29 American institutions. The majority of these degrees were Ph.D. degrees, but they included 17 Ped.D. degrees at New York University beginning in 1891, and four Sc.D. degrees at Cornell University beginning in 1895.[36]

From 1877 to 1959, 19,616 doctoral degrees of the research type were earned by women, or 12 percent of the total number of doctoral degrees conferred in the United States since 1861. The average number for the five years, 1955–59 was 920 per year. The total number through 1960, therefore, was well in excess of 21,000.

---

[35] *Alumnae Graduates School, Yale University, 1894–1920,* (New Haven, Conn.: Yale University, 1920), 78 pp. This volume contains biographical sketches of the 120 women.

[36] Walter Crosby Eells, "Earned Doctorates for Women in the Nineteenth Century," *AAUP Bulletin,* 42 (Winter, 1956), pp. 644–51. This article gives the names of each woman, degree, date, and institution. Titles of dissertations and other information concerning those in the fields of education, psychology, mathematics and astronomy, religion, modern languages, science, and English are given in later articles in *Educational Horizons,* 35 (Winter, 1956), pp. 53–6; *American Psychologist,* 12 (April, 1957), pp. 230–31; *Mathematics Teacher,* 50 (May, 1957), pp. 374–76; *Religious Education,* 52 (May-June, 1957), pp. 204–5; *Modern Language Journal,* 41 (May, 1957), pp. 209–11; *Science Education,* 41 (December, 1957), pp. 415–17; and *CLA Journal,* 2 (September, 1958), pp. 25–53.

The number at ten-year intervals since 1880, and percentages of total number, have been as follows:

Year	Number	Percentage of Total
1880	3	5.6%
1890	2	1.3
1900	22	5.8
1910	44	9.9
1920	93	15.1
1930	348	15.1
1940	429	13.0
1950	643	9.3
1960	1028	10.5

Note that although the number of doctorates earned by women has increased steadily, decade by decade, the proportion has not. The ten percent of women earning doctor's degrees in 1960 may be compared with the 32 percent who earned master's degrees and the 35 percent who earned bachelor's degrees the same year. The growing need for competent, well-trained college teachers suggests the desirability of a larger number of women completing their work for the doctorate in order to prepare themselves adequately for this important field of service.

Doctorates for Negroes

The first Ph.D. earned by a Negro was conferred by Yale University in 1876, just fifteen years after the same institution granted the first earned Ph.D. degrees in the United States. It was conferred on Edward Bouchet in physics with a dissertation "Measuring Refractive Indices." [37] He was also the first Negro to be elected to membership in Phi Beta Kappa.

---

[37] Harry W. Greene, *Holders of Doctorates Among American Negroes* (Boston, Mass.: Meador Publishing Co., 1946), p. 145. Greene (p. 22) erroneously gives the date of the first Ph.D. at Yale as 1866 instead of 1861. The report of the U.S. Commissioner of Education for 1873 states that Straight University, Louisiana (founded in 1869 and combined in 1930 with New Orleans University—also founded in 1869—to form the present Dillard University) conferred in 1873 two Ph.D. degrees, one honorary and one earned, thus distinguishing the two types. The same volume reports that the same year Straight had a faculty of four members and a total enrollment of 39 students, chiefly in the preparatory department, only 11 being college students—six freshmen and five sophomores. It is quite evident, therefore, that the earned Ph.D. reported in 1873 can scarcely be considered a true research doctorate, or the first Ph.D. earned by a Negro, in any acceptable sense.

Between 1876 and 1943 at least 381 persons of Negro descent (of whom 48 were women) earned research doctorates of various types. More than nine-tenths of these were Ph.D.'s, but there were also 18 Ed.D.'s, seven Doctor of Juridical Science, and five others in various fields. More than two-thirds of these degrees were conferred in the period 1935–43. They were conferred by 43 American and 14 foreign universities, the University of Chicago leading with 40. (These do not include professional doctorates in medicine and dentistry.)[38] Unfortunately, similar data for later years are not available.

In 1921 the first Negro women earned Ph.D. degrees: Sadie Tanner Mossell Alexander, University of Pennsylvania, economics; Eva Beatrice Dykes, Radcliffe College, English; and Georgiana Rose Simpson, University of Chicago, German. Rose Butler Browne at Harvard University and Virginia Romona Daniel at the University of Pittsburgh were the first Negro women to earn Ed.D. degrees, both in 1939.[39]

---

[38] *Ibid.*, pp. 22–42.
[39] *Ibid.*, pp. 50, 89, 93, 170, 176.

CHAPTER IV

The Doctor's Degree:
Professional Types

The Court doe therefore vnanimously enacte and declare that the said Captayne John Cranston . . . is by this Court styled and recorded Doctor of phissicke and chirurgery by the athority of the Generall Assembly of this Collony.

First American Doctor of Medicine, Rhode Island, 1664.[1]

The professional type of earned doctorates, as distinguished from the research type, are in American practice limited almost entirely to the medical and allied fields. Historically they had their academic origin in the latter part of the eighteenth century whereas the research type (see Chap. III) did not develop until after the middle of the nineteenth century. As first professional degrees they have been grouped with baccalaureate and other first level degrees in the annual statistical reports of the U. S. Office of Education. Beginning with 1961, however, the Office collected and published separately statistics for recipients of first professional degrees.

Medicine

As a matter of fact, when the earliest medical schools were established, there was no intention of conferring the relatively advanced degree of *Doctor* upon their graduates. The degree that was planned was the Bachelor of Medicine (B.M.), or, as it was originally designated, the Bachelor of Physic. Then after a suitable period of practice and advanced study the holder of this bachelor's degree was expected to return and receive the advanced degree of Doctor of Medicine. This was the system then in use in England. But this logical plan was rather short-lived in America.

The first class to secure degrees in medicine from an American school consisted of ten young men who completed their work for

---

[1] See footnote 7 for full reference.

the Bachelor of Physic at the College and Academy of Philadelphia (which later became a part of the present University of Pennsylvania). The secretary of the Board of the newly established Physic School proudly recorded in his minutes of June 21, 1768: "This day may be considered as the Birthday of Medical Honors in America." [2]

A later historian of the University, wrote: [3]

> In June 1768 a medical Commencement was held, separate from the rest of the College, at which, with much Latin disputation, and many orations by the prospective graduates, and much good advice by Provost and Vice-Provost, medical professors, and Trustees, ten young men were given the degree of Bachelor of Physic, the first medical degrees given in America. "An elegant Valedictory Oration," stating the advantages of obtaining a general liberal education before entering upon medical studies, was delivered by Jonathan Potts, one of the graduates.

The graduation of this pioneer class, however, was not accomplished without controversy—violent controversy that had nothing to do with the field of medicine but reflected the intense colonial patriotism of the time. This situation has been only recently reported in a publication of the University's School of Medicine: [4]

> John Archer's name comes down to us across two centuries as the first graduate of the first medical school in the New World. He's the ancestor of the medical profession in the United States, honored for receiving a truly unique degree in 1768 from what is now the University of Pennsylvania's School of Medicine. . . . It was June, seven years before the outbreak of the American Revolution, and ten young men had completed their studies, passed their examinations, and were qualified to receive the "Baccalaureate in Medicine" to be bestowed for the first time by the institution then known as the "College and Academy of Philadelphia." John Archer was one of the ten. And, since he possessed the further distinction of a name beginning with "A" he was the logical candidate to receive the first degree. Controversy arose because young Archer—though first on the list alphabetically—was born a Colonist and not an Englishman.

---

[2] William F. Norwood, *Medical Education in the United States Before the Civil War* (Philadelphia, Pa.: University of Pennsylvania Press, 1944), p. 68.

[3] Edwin P. Cheyney, *History of the University of Pennsylvania 1740–1940* (Philadelphia, Pa.: University of Pennsylvania Press, 1940), p. 103.

[4] "America's First Medical Graduate: John Archer, M.D.: Physician, Soldier, Patriot, Statesman," *Medical Affairs* (University of Pennsylvania School of Medicine and Graduate School of Medicine), Vol. 1, No. 3, Winter 1960, pp. 6–9.

The medical faculty, all of whom had received their medical education in England and Scotland, proposed to bestow the first honor on the single Englishman of the graduating group, a young man by the name of Potts. It took strong feeling—and strong action—on the part of the students to reverse the faculty stand. The rebel Colonial candidates eventually won the day by threatening to take their credentials, en masse, over the river to Princeton.

It may be speculated whether the valedictory honors for Mr. Potts reported in the previous quotation, may have been the result of some face-saving compromise!

Three years later, in 1771, the College of Philadelphia conferred the degree of M.B.[5] on a new group of seven students, and that of M.D. on four of the original ten who had constituted the first graduating class in 1768.

The second medical school in the New World was established at Columbia University (then known as King's College) in 1767. Like the University of Pennsylvania, it planned first to give the Bachelor of Physic degree, to be followed later by the doctorate. The requirements for the latter degree were thus stated: [6]

> In one Year after having obtained a Bachelor's Degree, a student may be admitted to his Examination for the *Degree* of Doctor, provided he shall have previously attended two Courses of Lectures under each Professor, be of Twenty-Two Years of Age, and have Published, and publicly defended, a Treatise upon some Medical Subject.

The first baccalaureate degrees under this plan were conferred on Robert Tucker and Samuel Kissam in 1769, and the first doctorates on the same two individuals in 1770 and 1771 respectively. Columbia therefore was the first college in America to confer the degree of *Doctor* of Medicine.

Rutgers University Medical School was organized in 1792 and discontinued in 1835. Its first class of three men received the M.B. degree in 1792, but the next class of six men in 1793—and all classes thereafter—received the M.D. degree directly.

The Harvard Medical School graduated 51 men with the B.M.

---

[5] Although the early degree, as stated above, was the Bachelor of Physic, it is recorded as Bachelor of Medicine in the latest published alumni catalogues of the various institutions concerned.

[6] *History of Columbia University, 1754–1904* (New York: Columbia University Press, 1904), pp. 311–12.

degree between 1788 and 1810, but only two of these took an M.D. degree, one in 1802, the other in 1810. In 1811, therefore, the degree of Doctor of Medicine was granted not only to graduates of that year, but retroactively to all earlier graduates who had not received it. All graduates since 1811 have received the M.D. degree.

In general, very few students in these early days, once they had graduated in medicine and were out in active practice, ever returned for the more advanced degree. Any man presumably competent to diagnose illness and prescribe remedies, particularly if he were a graduate of a medical school, was commonly known as a "doctor." Little or no attention was paid to the academic distinction between M.B. and M.D. The M.B. degree was therefore abandoned, by some institutions as early as 1790, and by most of them before 1812, although the Medical School of the University of Maryland continued to use it until 1848.

Advanced medical degrees are now chiefly the Doctor of Public Health and the Doctor of Medical Science (Med.Sc.D.). These degrees are classified with the Ph.D. and Ed.D. as advanced research degrees in the annual statistical reports of the U. S. Office of Education.

As a matter of historical interest at least one doctorate in the field of medicine, although possibly a borderline case between an earned and honorary degree, antedated John Archer and his nine fellow Pennsylvanians by more than a century. The distinction of conferring or at least authorizing this first medical degree in America belongs not to an educational institution but to the infant colony of Rhode Island. On March 1, 1664 when the Assembly of the new colony met, and less than a year after it was chartered by Charles II, the Assembly of the Colony of Rhode Island and Providence Plantations passed a legislative act which read: [7]

> Whereas the Court have taken notice of the great blessing of God on the good endevers of Captayne John Cranston of Newport, both in phissicke and chirurgery, to the great comfort of such as have had occation to improve his skill and practice &c. The Court doe therefore vnanimously enacte and declare that the said Captayne John Cranston is lycenced and commissioned to administer phissicke, and practice chirurgery throughout this whole Collony, and

[7] John Russell Bartlett, ed., *Records of the Colony of Rhode Island and Providence Plantations in New England* (Providence, R.I.: A. Crawford Greene and Brother, 1857), Vol. II, 1664–1677, p. 33.

is by this Court styled and recorded Doctor of phisick and chirurgery by the athority of the General Assembly of this Collony.

It has already been pointed out that if the legislature of a state or
colony has the power to authorize an educational institution to confer a degree, it has itself the power to confer a degree. Thus almost
a century and a half later, in December 1807, the General Assembly
of the State of Maryland conferred M.D. degrees on three men, all
members of the first faculty of the College of Medicine of Maryland.
It is probable, however, that these three Maryland degrees should be
listed as honorary degrees, whereas the Rhode Island action is
harder to classify, since it appears to be a recognition of ability and
right to practice medicine at a time when no educational institution
could give this right.

Another noneducational agency which conferred medical degrees
in early years was the Connecticut State Medical Society. Its charter
gave it the right to confer the M.D. degree and it granted 36 such
degrees from 1793 to 1813. Then it joined with Yale in organizing
and conducting the Yale Medical Institution, later the Yale School
of Medicine, and transferred to Yale College its function of conferring degrees.[8] This joint responsibility was not dissolved until
1884, when the University assumed full control.

Although Columbia University granted the first earned Doctor of
Medicine in 1770, this degree was conferred as an honorary degree
upon the English physician, Daniel Turner, almost a half century
earlier by the recently established Yale College (see Chap. V).

In 1961 there were 81 approved medical schools in the United
States, all conducting a complete course of study, four years or more
in length, leading to the M.D. degree.

Medical degrees for women. The first professional doctor's degree in medicine earned by a woman was the M.D. conferred on
Elizabeth Blackwell (1821–1910) in 1849 by the Medical Institution of Geneva, New York, now the College of Medicine of Syracuse
University. She attended this institution for two years, after being
refused admission to medical schools in Philadelphia, New York,
and Boston. Miss Blackwell, whose father had brought her to New
York from England when she was eleven years of age, returned to

---

[8] Frederick C. Waite, "Medical Degrees Conferred in the American Colonies
and in the United States in the Eighteenth Century," *Annals of Medical History*,
9 (July, 1937), pp. 316–319.

Europe after securing her M.D. degree for further medical study in London and Paris. She then returned to America and with her sister Emily (1826–1910), who had secured an M.D. from Western Reserve University in 1854. In 1857, they established in New York, in spite of much opposition, a hospital staffed entirely by women and offering a full course of instruction; the New York Infirmary and College for Women. In 1869 she returned to England and in 1875 helped to found the London School of Medicine for Women.[9]

Dentistry

The first dental school in the United States, if not in the world, was the Baltimore College of Dental Surgery, an independent institution, organized in 1840 (and merged with University of Maryland in 1923), which conferred the degree of Doctor of Dental Surgery (D.D.S.) on two men in 1841. This was the first use of this degree by an educational institution. But earlier the American Society of Dental Surgeons had formally sanctioned the use of the title "Dental Surgeon" and had conferred on its members, by what authority is not clear, the degree of Doctor of Dental Surgery.[10] It may be noted that this was long after the attempt to confer the Bachelor of Medicine on the graduates of medical schools. It had become accepted as a general principle that the graduate of a school in any of the health-related fields was entitled to the title and degree of "Doctor."

The first dental school to be connected with a university was the Dental School of Harvard University, established in 1869, which offered the degree of Doctor of Dental Medicine (D.M.D.). By 1960 all accredited dental schools, 45 in number, were associated with universities.

The Association of American Universities in 1924 adopted unanimously the recommendations of its Committee on Higher Academic and Professional Degrees concerning degrees in dentistry. The Committee recommended the degree of Doctor of Dental Surgery as preferable to Doctor of Dental Science, although its chairman suggested Harvard's Doctor of Dental Medicine as preferable to either.

---

[9] For details of her early work in medicine, see her *Pioneer Work in Opening the Medical Profession to Women: Autobiographical Sketches* (London and New York: Longmans, Green and Co., 1895), 265 pp.

[10] William J. Gies, *Dental Education in the United States and Canada* (New York: Carnegie Foundation for the Advancement of Teaching, 1926), p. 72.

In 1960, use of the degrees Doctor of Dental Surgery was reported by 38 dental schools, Doctor of Dental Medicine by six, and Doctor of Dental Science by one.

Between 1840 and 1960, 153,000 individuals received degrees from dental schools. By 1961 the rate was about 3,400 annually.[11]

Veterinary Medicine

The first generally recognized institution in the United States for training veterinarians was the New York College of Veterinary Surgeons, chartered in 1857 and reorganized in 1864. In 1867 it awarded the degree of Veterinary Surgeon (V.S.) to two men. Cornell University began offering courses in veterinary medicine in 1868. In 1872 it granted the degree of Bachelor of Veterinary Science (B.V.S.) to Daniel E. Salmon who, after a period of clinical study in Europe, was given the degree of Doctor of Veterinary Medicine (D.V.M.)—undoubtedly the first such doctorate to be conferred in America.

The American Veterinary College, organized in 1875, granted the degree of Doctor of Veterinary Surgery (D.V.S.) to a class of 18 men in 1876.[12]

The first formal education in veterinary medicine was about 1740 in France. The first English college of veterinary medicine was established in London in 1791.[13]

At present the degree of Doctor of Veterinary Medicine (D.V.M.) is offered by 16 institutions in the United States.

Pharmacy

In the earlier part of the nineteenth century the degree of Doctor of Pharmacy (Pharm.D.) was used by some proprietary schools of pharmacy without adequate standards and as a result it became cheapened and discredited. It was first used by a recognized institu-

---

[11] Mary Irwin, ed., *American Universities and Colleges,* 8th ed. (Washington, D.C.: American Council on Education, 1960), p. 87.

[12] Walter C. Eells and Harold A. Haswell, *Academic Degrees: Earned and Honorary Degrees Conferred by Institutions of Higher Education in the United States* (Washington, D.C.: U.S. Department of Health, Education, and Welfare: Office of Education, 1960), p. 166; based on personal letter from Dr. J. F. Smithcors, College of Veterinary Medicine, Michigan State University, March 9, 1960.

[13] Mary Irwin, *op. cit.,* p. 148.

tion of high standing, the Philadelphia College of Pharmacy (now the Philadelphia College of Pharmacy and Science), in 1895.

In 1960, however, the doctor's degree was used by only five of the accredited schools of pharmacy. Most of the 78 accredited schools of pharmacy offer the Bachelor of Science in Pharmacy (B.S. Pharm.) as their first degree, a few the simpler Bachelor of Pharmacy (B.Pharm.).[14] Such graduates are not entitled to use the title "Doctor," although many of them are so addressed, through courtesy or ignorance.

Other Professional Doctorates

Various other professional doctorates not of the research type are found in a variety of medical fields and are offered by a few institutions. These include Doctor of Surgical Chiropody (offered in 1960 by four institutions), Doctor of Chiropractic (four), Doctor of Optometry (six), Doctor of Osteopathy (five), and Doctor of Podiatry (one).

In 1876 Yale University established advanced courses in law and political science leading to a degree of Doctor of Civil Law, but this degree is now given only as an honorary degree.

---

[14] Walter C. Eells and Harold A. Haswell, *op. cit.,* pp. 183–86.

CHAPTER V

The Doctor's Degree:
Honorary Types

> Honorary degrees are in some institutions, and not usually those
> of the highest standing, conferred with a profuseness which seems
> to argue an exaggerated appreciation of inconspicuous merit.
>
> James Bryce, in *The American Commonwealth,* 1888 [1]

Honorary degrees are usually conferred at Commencement or on
special anniversary occasions, in recognition of distinguished public
service or outstanding creative work. Like many other phases of
American academic practice they were patterned on British university usage, but extended and adapted to American conditions and
needs. In place of the orders of nobility and royal lists of honors
that are found in England, they form in the American democracy a
distinctive method of recognizing outstanding service or achievement.[2]

Unfortunately, however, honorary doctorates and—to a lesser extent—honorary master's and bachelor's degrees as well have been
widely used and sometimes abused by American universities and
colleges. They have sometimes been given for thinly disguised com-
mercial considerations, for publicity, or for the satisfaction of personal vanity. Such questionable uses, however, represent only the
abuse of the honorary degree principle, which on the whole serves a
useful and desirable place in American public life.

---

[1] James Bryce, *The American Commonwealth* (London: Macmillan, 1888),
p. 538.

[2] See Bernard N. Schilling, "The Public Orator and Graduation *Honoris Causa,*"
AAUP Bulletin, 45 (June, 1959), pp. 260–71, for an account of uses and abuses
of honorary degrees in England. See Stephen Edward Epler, *Honorary Degrees:
A Survey of Their Use and Abuse* (Washington, D.C.: American Council on
Public Affairs, 1943), 224 pp., based upon doctoral dissertation at Columbia
University, for full discussion of honorary degrees chiefly at seven institutions:
Harvard, Columbia, Smith College, and Universities of North Carolina, Wisconsin,
Nebraska, and California. See also "Under What Conditions Confer Honorary
Degrees?" National Association of State Universities, *Proceedings,* 1936, pp. 158–
74.

Honorary Doctorates Before the Revolution

Honorary doctorates were rarely conferred by American colleges before the Revolutionary War. Of the nine colonial colleges which were chartered before 1776, apparently only five—Harvard, Yale, Princeton, Columbia, and Dartmouth [3]—according to their alumni catalogues conferred a total of 28 honorary doctorates before 1776. One of these was granted in 1692, one in 1723, and all the others in the decade immediately preceding 1776.[4]

Columbia conferred the largest number, nine; Princeton, seven; Harvard, five; Dartmouth, four; and Yale, three. The first honorary Doctor of Sacred Theology (S.T.D.) was conferred by Harvard in 1692. The first honorary M.D. was conferred by Yale in 1723. Columbia conferred the first honorary Doctor of Laws (LL.D.) in

---

[3] At this period Princeton was the College of New Jersey; Columbia was King's College. Present names of these and other institutions are used here and usually elsewhere for convenience of present identification.

[4]

HARVARD	1692	S.T.D.	Increase Mather
(1636)	1771	S.T.D.	Nathaniel Appleton
	1773	S.T.D.	Samuel Locke
	1773	S.T.D.	Samuel Mather
	1773	LL.D.	John Winthrop
YALE	1723	M.D.	Daniel Turner
(1701)	1773	LL.D.	Richard Jackson
	1774	D.D.	Benjamin Lord (or S.T.D.)
PRINCETON	1769	LL.D.	John Dickinson
(1746)	1769	LL.D.	Joseph Galloway
	1770	D.D.	Archibald Laidlie
	1772	D.D.	Daniel Fisher
	1773	D.D.	Samuel Wilton
	1774	D.D.	Naphtali Daggett
	1774	D.D.	Noah Welles
COLUMBIA	1767	S.T.D.	Samuel Auchmuty
(1754)	1767	S.T.D.	Thomas B. Chandler
	1768	M.D.	Samuel Bard
	1768	M.D.	Samuel Classy
	1768	LL.D.	Myles Cooper
	1768	M.D.	John Jones
	1768	M.D.	Peter Middleton
	1770	LL.D.	John Ogilvie
	1774	D.C.L.	William Tryon (or LL.D.)
DARTMOUTH	1773	D.D.	Samuel Haven
(1769)	1773	LL.D.	John Wentworth
	1773	D.D.	Stephen Williams
	1774	D.D.	Benjamin Pomeroy

1768, and the first Doctor of Civil Law (D.C.L.) in 1774. Dartmouth granted the first honorary D.D. in 1773. (S.T.D. degrees are sometimes referred to as D.D. degrees, but the two are distinct. Similarly, D.C.L. and LL.D. are sometimes confused.) Honorary D.D. degrees were given to nine men before 1776; LL.D. degrees to seven; S.T.D. degrees to six; M.D. degrees to five; and D.C.L. degrees to one.

Comments concerning some of the individuals honored with doctorates before 1776, especially those about whom some controversy has developed, may be of interest.

Increase Mather (1639–1723). The first man to receive an honorary doctorate (the S.T.D.) from an American educational institution—and the only one to be so honored in the seventeenth century—was Increase Mather, sixth president of Harvard College.[5] In 1692, the College, acting almost immediately upon the provision of the Harvard charter of 1692 (which it assumed would be approved by the British Privy Council), not only conferred the honorary doctorate upon its president, but also granted honorary degrees of Bachelor of Sacred Theology (S.T.B.) upon the two tutors. Thus the entire faculty of the young institution had the prestige of academic degrees beyond the baccalaureate.

Dr. Samuel E. Morison, the distinguished Harvard historian, says that these were not honorary degrees nor *ad eundem* degrees.[6] He says that Mather, as a dissenter, was not eligible for a divinity degree at Oxford or Cambridge. Nevertheless the official Harvard *Quinquennial Catalogue* lists these degrees as honorary degrees, not earned degrees. It may be noted, too, that this doctorate was not given to Mather when he became president of Harvard in 1685 as might have been expected, but seven years later, when he had achieved considerable distinction independent of his Harvard presidency. It was conferred immediately after he had spent four years in London as an official agent of the Colony and had succeeded in

---

[5] Of the five earlier presidents of Harvard, the first two, Henry Dunster (president, 1640–54), and Charles Chauncy (1654–72) were graduates of the University of Cambridge; Leonard Hoar (1672–75) had an A.B. from Harvard in 1650 and an M.D. from Cambridge in 1671; Uriah Oakes (1675–81), and John Rogers (1682–84), had only A.B. degrees from Harvard, both in 1649, followed by the customary A.M.

[6] Samuel Eliot Morison, *Harvard College in the Seventeenth Century* (Cambridge, Mass.: Harvard University Press, 1936), p. 491.

having the new colonial charter of 1691 modified greatly to the advantage of the colony. Although it is true that he was not eligible for a divinity degree at Oxford or Cambridge, he did receive an M.A. degree from Trinity College, Dublin, in 1658, two years after he had received his A.B. from Harvard. Although he was forced from the presidency of Harvard in 1701 because of political repercussions growing out of the new colonial charter, he continued his interest in public and church affairs. A biographer says he was "the most powerful man of his time in the Puritan Colonies." [7] He published more than 150 books, in theology, history, biography, and science. It would seem that he was fully worthy of an honorary doctorate in 1692. Furthermore, the text of his diploma indicates that the degree was given him because of his many books, which proved him to be highly versed "not only in the Tongues and Liberal Arts, but in the Holy Scriptures and Theology," and "because he had rendered himself for his Learning and Merits, the object of highest commendation, not only among the American but among the European Churches." [8]

Appleton, Locke, Mather. These three men, who were also granted honorary S.T.D. degrees by Harvard, were eminent clergymen of Massachusetts. Samuel Mather was the grandson of Increase Mather. Samuel Locke was president of Harvard from 1770 to 1773, and received his honorary doctorate in the last year of his presidency.

John Winthrop (1714–1779). Harvard's first honorary LL.D. (see p. 54) was conferred in 1773 on John Winthrop, who served as second Hollis Professor of Mathematics at the College for more than 40 years (during which time he introduced the study of calculus) and was an eminent astronomer and physicist as well. (For erroneous statements regarding Harvard's *first* LL.D. degree, see p. 61.) He was also a Fellow of the Harvard Corporation, and was twice elected to the presidency of Harvard—in 1769 and 1774— but declined both times. He was elected a Fellow of the Royal Society in 1766 and in 1771 had already received an honorary LL.D.

---

[7] Kenneth B. Murdock, "Increase Mather," in *Encyclopaedia Britannica.*

[8] S. E. Morison, *op. cit.,* p. 492. For further discussion of question of whether President Mather's was an honorary degree, see articles by S. E. Morison in *Harvard Alumni Bulletin,* June 15, 1934; and by Kimball C. Elkins in *Harvard Library Bulletin,* Autumn, 1958.

from the University of Edinburgh. The LL.D. degree hardly seems appropriate for a man of such eminence in scientific fields, but the honorary degree of Sc.D. was not then in use.

Daniel Turner (1667–1741). Several facts are of special interest concerning the honorary M.D. degree granted to Daniel Turner in 1723. This was the first honorary degree conferred by Yale College, only twenty years after its first baccalaureate degree. It may be wondered why the recently established college, which had no school of medicine until almost a century later, should have awarded any type of medical degree in the early eighteenth century, and particularly to a British physician who was not a resident of Connecticut and who never even visited the New World.

In that period most of the British physicians were graduates of Oxford or Cambridge or of one of the Scottish universities. At that time the standards of the Scottish medical faculties were notoriously low. Turner had published a book *The Modern Quack* (1718) in which he vigorously attacked the Scottish universities for their shameful practice of virtually selling medical diplomas, and for their other discreditable policies. He was therefore *persona non grata* at those institutions, and since he was not a member of the Church of England, was not eligible for a degree from an English university. But he needed a degree in order to be eligible for election to the Royal Society of Physicians and Surgeons.

It happened that Turner had come to the favorable attention of Jeremiah Dummer, who had gone to London in 1712 as colonial agent for Connecticut, and who was interested in the development of the recently established Yale. At Dummer's suggestion, therefore, Turner applied to Yale for a medical degree (his original letter in Latin and an English translation of it are in the Yale library). His letter was transmitted to the Yale authorities by Dummer, who described some of Turner's books, commented highly on their value, and closed, "If you send this Gentleman a Diploma for a Doctorate, you will do yourselves great honour." On the basis of Dummer's recommendation, therefore, the desired degree was conferred as an honorary M.D. *in absentia,* on September 11, 1723.[9]

---

[9] John E. Lane, "Daniel Turner and the First Degree of Doctor of Medicine Conferred in the English Colonies of North America by Yale College in 1723," *Annals of Medical History,* 2 (Winter, 1919), pp. 367–81.

Dexter's well known sketches of Yale graduates describes Dr. Turner's honorary degree as follows: [10]

> An honorary degree of Doctor of Medicine was conferred upon Dr. Daniel Turner, a well-known Fellow of the Royal College of Physicians in London, who had accompanied his letters soliciting the honor with a gift of twenty-eight volumes of valuable medical books (several of them written by himself); the circumstance that the degree was thus prefaced led some wit of the period to declare that the mystic letters, "M.D.," must mean *"Multum Donavit."*

It appears, therefore, that the practice of conferring an honorary degree at least partly as recognition of a special gift, which has served to debase the honor in more recent years, had an ancient precedent.

Tryon, Ogilvie. William Tryon was the British Colonial Governor of New York and John Ogilvie was a clergyman of the Church of England. Governor Tryon received his honorary degree, D.C.L., on March 29, 1774 and a week later, April 6, made a grant of 10,000 acres of land in Vermont to his new Alma Mater. The intervention of the war, however, prevented the actual transfer of title.[11] A loyalist, Tryon fled to England, never to return. According to the *Dictionary of American Biography* he was "one of the most detested Loyalists in New York."

John Wentworth. Sir John Wentworth was the last Royal governor of New Hampshire. In 1769, he granted a charter to Dartmouth College. Later he conferred grants of land to the new institution and devoted time and personal attention to its affairs. He was a member of the first board of trustees. As a Loyalist, however, he fled to England during the Revolution. He was later appointed Lieutenant Governor of Halifax, 1792–1808.[12]

---

[10] Franklin Bowditch Dexter, *Biographical Sketches of the Graduates of Yale College with Annals of the College History. Vol. 1, October 1701–May 1745* (New York: Henry Holt and Company, 1885), p. 274.

[11] John B. Pine, "A Forgotten Benefactor," *Columbia University Quarterly,* 10 (March, 1908), pp. 148–53. The Columbia alumni catalogue gives the degree as LL.D., as does Epler, (p. 10) and others. But Fine gives the complete laudatory citation in full, in the original Latin, which clearly states his degree as "Juris Civilis Doctorum." Epler also confuses the dates of the two events, making them only a day apart.

[12] *Dictionary of American Biography* (New York: Charles Scribner's Sons, 1937), Vol. 19, pp. 656–57.

Other Honorary Doctorates in the Eighteenth Century

Although relatively few honorary doctorates were conferred from 1642 to 1774, the number increased markedly in the last quarter of the century.

Prior to 1776, many outstanding individuals in the American colonies had received honorary doctorates from British universities, the most notable, perhaps, being Benjamin Franklin, who received an LL.D. from the University of St. Andrews in 1759 and a D.C.L. from the University of Oxford in 1762. But this source of honorary degrees, understandably, almost vanished after 1776. Some American institutions too were not entirely sure of their right to confer honorary degrees or at least of the propriety of their doing so, since this was a university function in England and there were no true universities in the American colonies at that time.

But as soon as political independence was asserted, American colleges began to assert greater academic independence as well. They no longer had to fear possible vetoes of their awards by the British Privy Council. They began to confer honorary degrees much more liberally, in order to honor outstanding leaders in the War for Independence and to give additional academic prestige to their faculties, particularly those of the newly established schools of medicine.

From 1776 to 1800 at least 258 honorary doctorates were conferred by the following institutions: [13]

Institutions (In order of founding)	Total	LL.D.	D.D.	S.T.D.	M.D.
Harvard	60	20	—	21	19
William and Mary	14	5	8	—	1
Yale	16	8	4	—	4
Princeton	52	20	32	—	—
Columbia	10	2	—	8	—
Pennsylvania	26	9	17	—	—
Brown	33	20	13	—	—
Rutgers	10	1	3	—	6
Dartmouth	30	17	10	—	3
Washington (Md.)	1	1	—	—	—
Union	4	2	2	—	—
University of State of N.Y. (State Educ. Dept.)	2	2	—	—	—
Total	258	107	89	29	33

[13] Compiled from alumni catalogues of the various institutions, but such catalogues were not available for five of the smaller institutions, chartered after

Many of these honorary doctorates were conferred on men, both American and French, who had played important parts in the struggle for independence. The individual who was thus honored more than any one else was, quite appropriately, George Washington, who received honorary LL.D. degrees from Harvard in 1776, from Yale in 1781, from Pennsylvania in 1783, from Washington College (named in his honor), Maryland, in 1784, and from Brown in 1790. In March 1776, while what remained of Harvard was existing in temporary refugee quarters in Concord, the British were forced to evacuate Boston. To signalize this important event, the Harvard Corporation and a handful of Overseers met at Watertown on April 3 and voted to confer on Washington the honorary degree commonly reported as Doctor of Laws, but actually the more generous inclusive degree of "Doctor of Laws, the Law of Nature and of Nations, and the Civil Law," probably the most comprehensive honorary degree ever awarded by any American institution. The group called on Washington the same day (presumably at his Cambridge headquarters in Craigie House), conferred the degree, and presented the diploma [14] which, in accordance with the custom of the day, was in Latin. The English translation of it reads as follows:

The CORPORATION OF HARVARD COLLEGE in Cambridge, in New-England, to all the faithful in Christ, to whom these Presents shall come, GREETING.

WHEREAS Academical Degrees were originally instituted for this Purpose, That Men, eminent for Knowledge, Wisdom and Virtue, who have highly merited of the Republick of Letters and the Common-Wealth, should be rewarded with the Honor of the Laurels; there is the greatest Propriety in conferring such Honor on that very illustrous Gentleman, GEORGE WASHINGTON, Esq.; the accomplished General of the confederated Colonies in America; whose knowledge and patriotic Ardor are manifest to all: Who, for his distinguished Virtues, both Civil and Military, in the first Place being elected by the Suffrages of the Virginians, one of their Delegates, exerted himself with Fidelity and singular Wisdom in the cele-

---

1780, which had their first commencements before 1801. Probably few, if any, of them conferred any honorary doctorates before that date.

[14] Samuel Eliot Morison, *Three Centuries of Harvard, 1636–1936* (Cambridge, Mass.: Harvard University Press, 1936), p. 150. Washington's diploma was printed, both in Latin and in English, in the Boston papers. The Latin text is given in Josiah Quincy, *History of Harvard University* (Boston, Mass.: Crosby, Nichols, Lee, & Co., 1848), Vol. II, 506–7. The English text is given in *Publications of the Colonial Society of Massachusetts, Volume 7, Transactions, 1900–1902* (Boston, Mass., The Society, 1905), pp. 328–29.

brated *Congress of America,* for the Defense of Liberty, when in the utmost Danger of being forever lost, and for the Salvation of his Country; and then, at the earnest Request of that Grand Council of Patriots, without Hesitation, left all the Pleasures of his delightful Seat in Virginia, and the Affairs of his own Estate, that through all the Fatigues and Dangers of a Camp, without accepting any Reward, he might deliver *New-England* from the unjust and cruel Arms of Britain, and defend the other Colonies; and Who, by the most signal Smiles of Divine Providence on his Military Operations, drove the Fleet and Troops of the Enemy with disgraceful Precipitation from the Town of Boston, which for eleven Months had been shut up, fortified, and defended by a Garrison of above seven Thousand Regulars; so that the Inhabitants, who suffered a great Variety of Hardships and Cruelties while under the Power of their Oppressors, now rejoice in their Deliverance, the neighboring Towns are freed from the Tumults of Arms, and our University has the agreeable Prospect of being restored to its ancient Seat.

Know ye therefore, that We, the President and Fellows of Harvard-College in Cambridge, (with the Consent of the Honored and Reverend Overseers of our Academy) have constituted and created the aforesaid Gentleman, GEORGE WASHINGTON, who merits the highest Honor, Doctor of Laws, the Law of Nature and Nations, and the Civil Law; and have given and granted him at the same Time all Rights, Privileges, and Honors, to the said Degree pertaining.

In Testimony whereof, We have affixed the Common Seal of our University to these Letters, and subscribed them with our Hand writing this Third Day of April in the Year of our Lord one Thousand seven Hundred Seventy-six.

The Latin of the degree was *Doctor Utriusque Juris, tum Naturae et Gentium, tum Civilis.* The last phrase is redundant since *Utriusque* "Doctor of Both Laws" or simply "Doctor of Laws" included both canon law and civil law. But the Harvard president and fellows evidently wanted to give George Washington the best they had— and to spare.

Although President Quincy of Harvard in 1840, and other writers over the next half century, asserted unequivocally that George Washington was the first person to receive an honorary LL.D. degree from Harvard, Harvard had conferred this degree on John Winthrop three years earlier (see pp. 54, 56).[15] In fact, Washing-

---

[15] Josiah Quincy, *op. cit.,* p. 167. "General Washington was the first individual on whom this degree was conferred by Harvard College." Equivalent statements by Samuel A. Eliot, *Sketch of the History of Harvard College and of Its Present State* (Boston, Mass.: Charles C. Little & James Brown, 1848), p. 83; and by

ton's diploma was signed by one of the Fellows, "Johannes Winthrop, LL.D."

In 1784 Harvard also conferred honorary LL.D. degrees on three Frenchmen who had given significant assistance in the Revolution. The best known was the Marquis de Lafayette who, at the age of 27, was the youngest man ever to receive this degree from Harvard, if not indeed from any American institution.

In 1782 the College of William and Mary conferred honorary LL.D. degrees upon Thomas Jefferson, and upon a general and a physician in the French army who had been prominent in Virginia in the later years of the Revolution.

Honorary Doctorates Since 1800

There are few records of honorary doctorates conferred during the first half of the nineteenth century, except in scattered alumni catalogs and similar institutional records which have never been compiled on any national basis.

The granting of honorary M.D. degrees became almost a scandal between 1830 and 1860. When the American Medical Association was founded in 1846, one thing it did was to attempt to stop the excessive flow of honorary medical degrees, and it succeeded—at least in part.[16]

The first honorary degree of Doctor of Music was conferred on Henry Dielman by Georgetown University, Washington, D. C., in 1849 at Commencement exercises made notable by the attendance of President Zachary Taylor, who awarded the degrees. Dr. Dielman served as head of the music department of St. Mary's University, Maryland, for forty years.

In 1875, John Eaton, Jr., second U. S. Commissioner of Education, summarized the situation regarding honorary degrees, especially doctorates, and uttered a word of caution: [17]

> American colleges are much in the habit of giving honorary degrees. This practice, copied from the two greatest English uni-

Albert Bushnell Hart, in *Harvard Graduates Magazine*, 9, p. 516, and by Albert Bushnell Hart, "The University: Reflections and Problems," *Harvard Graduates Magazine*, 9 (June 1901), pp. 506–17. For full discussion and corrections by Henry H. Edes, see *Publications of the Colonial Society of Massachusetts, op. cit.,* pp. 322–24.

[16] Stephen Epler, *op. cit.,* p. 16.

[17] U. S. Commissioner of Education, *Annual Report,* 1877, p. cvii.

versities, has been carried on without due discrimination. It is confined almost entirely to the colleges proper; no school of theology during the year 1875 gave any honorary doctorate of divinity; no school of law conferred any honorary doctorate of law; only five honorary doctorates of medicine were conferred by the medical schools. The colleges gave honorary doctorates as follows: 138 in divinity, D.D.; 2 in medicine, M.D.; 68 in law, LL.D.; 19 in philosophy, Ph.D.; and 4 in music, Mus.D. They also conferred 130 honorary masterships of arts. It is true that most of these degrees were conferred on men who had graduated from college and that most of the recipients were professional men, but the practice is one very liable to abuse and is discountenanced now by some of the leading schools.

It may be noted that less than two-thirds of the honorary degrees reported by the Commissioner in 1875 were doctorates. In the entire period from 1872 to 1900, 65 percent of the honorary degrees conferred were doctorates, but in the twentieth century the proportion has been much greater. In the period from 1872 to 1900, the proportions of the doctorates conferred were D.D., 59 percent; LL.D., 29 percent; Ph.D., seven percent; others five percent. Of the "others" the most frequently found were Sc.D., L.H.D., and Litt.D., but with less than one percent for each.[18]

In 1916 the Commissioner of Education reported the number of doctorates conferred that year as LL.D., 293; D.D., 282; Sc.D., 51; Litt. D., 43; L.H.D., 16; Ped.D., 10; and ten others, 16.

The New York State Department of Education (officially the University of the State of New York) is the only state education department which for more than a century has consistently conferred honorary doctorates at its regular annual convocations. From 1792 to 1960 it conferred 127 honorary doctorates, distributed as follows: LL.D., 67; Ph.D. (from 1860 to 1890 only), 30; L.H.D., 18; Sc.D., six; Litt.D., five; D.C.L., one. All except two of these were conferred after 1828.[19]

The record for the largest number of doctorates received by any one man is undoubtedly held by ex-President Herbert Hoover. According to *Who's Who in America,* he has received this honor from

---

18 Stephen Epler, *op. cit.,* p. 47.

19 Albert B. Corey, Hugh M. Flick, and Frederick A. Morse, *The Regents of the University of the State of New York, 1784–1959* (Albany, N.Y.: The University of the State of New York, The State Education Department, 1959), p. 47.

no fewer than 81 educational institutions in the United States and abroad.

In 1960 all institutions in the United States were asked to report the *different* doctoral degrees which they had conferred "within recent years." They reported more than 120 different honorary doctorates. The degrees conferred by ten or more institutions, and the number of institutions granting them, are listed below: [20]

Degree	*Number of Institutions*
Doctor of Laws	449
Doctor of Humane Letters	310
Doctor of Divinity	308
Doctor of Science	221
Doctor of Literature	210
Doctor of Letters	111
Doctor of Music	102
Doctor of Humanities	52
Doctor of Engineering	47
Doctor of Fine Arts	33
Doctor of Commercial Science	22
Doctor of Education	22
Doctor of Pedagogy	22
Doctor of Sacred Theology	19
Doctor of Civil Law	16
Doctor of Business Administration	11

Ph.D. as an Honorary Degree

The longest and most intense struggle to develop and protect the academic standing of any doctorate has revolved about the Ph.D. degree. Although it was first conferred as an earned degree at Yale University in 1861, it was awarded as an honorary degree at least as early as 1852 when Bucknell University conferred it on E. N. Elliott. Bucknell also conferred it on seven other men before 1861 and on nine more by 1893.[21] Princeton conferred its first honorary Ph.D. in 1866 and 67 before 1896, during which period it granted only twenty earned Ph.D.'s.[22] (This is probably the record for any

---

[20] Walter Crosby Eells and Harold A. Haswell, *Academic Degrees: Earned and Honorary Degrees Conferred by Institutions of Higher Education in the United States* (Washington, D.C.: U. S. Department of Health, Education, and Welfare: Office of Education, 1960), p. 47.

[21] *Bucknell University Alumni Catalog, 1851–1915* (Lewisburg, Pa., 1915), p. 13.

[22] Stephen Epler, *op. cit.*, p. 59.

nineteenth century institution.) On the other hand, Harvard and Columbia have never conferred the Ph.D. as an honorary degree.

Reports of the U.S. Commissioner of Education indicate that honorary Ph.D. degrees were conferred on more than 700 individuals between 1872 and 1900 by over 100 different institutions. In 1874, 1875, 1876, 1879, and 1881, more honorary than earned Ph.D. degrees were reported. After 1900 the number of honorary ones decreased, but the records of the U. S. Office of Education (incomplete after 1918) show that at least 170 and probably more than 200 honorary Ph.D.'s were conferred by American institutions of higher education from 1901 to 1937.[23] The last one was conferred on Harry L. (Bing) Crosby, of Hollywood fame, by Gonzaga University, Spokane, Washington, in 1937.[24] Thus for at least 85 years, from 1852 to 1937, the Ph.D. was conferred by some universities as an honorary degree.

The first organized protest against the honorary Ph.D. came from the American Philological Association at its meeting in Cincinnati in 1881. At this meeting the following resolution was presented: [25]

> *Whereas,* many colleges in the United States have in recent years conferred the degree of Doctor of Philosophy not by examination but *honoris causa,* be it
>
> *Resolved, first,* That this Association deprecates the removal of this degree from the class to which it belongs (namely B.D., LL.B., M.D., and Ph.D.—degrees conferred after examination) and its transfer to the class of honorary degrees.
>
> *Secondly,* That a committee of three be appointed to present this resolution to the American Association for the Advancement of Science, and to request them to co-operate with this Association in addressing a memorial to the Boards of Trustees of all colleges in the United States empowered to confer degrees, stating the objections to conferring the degree of Doctor of Philosophy *honoris causa,* and praying them to discontinue the practice if it exists in the colleges under their control.

---

[23] Walter Crosby Eells, "Honorary Ph.D.'s in the 20th Century," *School and Society,* 85 (March 2, 1957), pp. 74–5.

[24] Eells and Haswell, *op. cit.,* p. 45, report that the last honorary Ph.D. was conferred by Providence College, Rhode Island, in 1959. But after this statement had been given wide newspaper publicity, the president of the institution wrote that an error had been made by his registrar's office in reporting an honorary LL.D. as a Ph.D. For correction see 1961 edition of the same work, p. 52. It may be noted that an honorary Ph.D. was conferred on an American educator by a Japanese university in the late 1950's.

[25] American Philological Association, *Proceedings,* 1881, p. 4.

This resolution was referred to the Executive Committee and at a later session after some discussion of the propriety of the Association taking such action during which it was stated that "there were no non-local organizations in the country from which such a protest could come with more propriety or with less danger of invidious reception," the resolution was passed and the following implementing committee named: John Williams White, Harvard, Chairman; Charles R. Lanham, Harvard; and Irving J. Manatt, Marietta College, Ohio.[26]

The American Association for the Advancement of Science concurred in this resolution at its annual meeting later the same year. At this meeting vigorous criticism was expressed of the "indiscriminate and lavish way in which the Doctor of Philosophy and Doctor of Science were conferred as honorary degrees," instead of as "earned rewards for scientific work and high attainments in philosophic study." [27]

A strong attack on the use of the Ph.D. as an honorary degree was made by Charles F. Smith, Professor of Greek at Nashville University, at the meeting of the National Education Association in 1889. This address was later published and widely circulated by the U.S. Office of Education. Professor Smith related several specific examples of recent degradation of the degree, and noted with regret the spread of the practice to many of the smaller colleges: [28]

> It is a pity that the custom has not been confined to small colleges, for then it might easily be rendered ridiculous, and so checked; but when such a protest as that of the philological and scientific associations is unheeded by institutions like Princeton, Amherst, Michigan University, Lafayette, Dartmouth, Hamilton, Madison, Union, Dickinson, Western Reserve, University of Wisconsin, University of North Carolina, DePauw, University of the City of New York, all of which conferred Ph.D. as an honorary degree the year after the protest or later, it cannot be hoped that the weaker institutions, West, South, or East, will seriously heed the protests of the scholars.

In 1890, William T. Harris, in his first report as U. S. Commis-

---

[26] *Ibid.,* p. 16.

[27] Edgar W. Knight, "Getting Ahead by Degrees," *School and Society,* 53 (April 26, 1941), pp. 524–28. See also American Association for the Advancement of Science, *Proceedings,* 1881, p. 522.

[28] Charles Forster Smith, *Honorary Degrees as Conferred in American Colleges* (Washington, D.C.: U.S. Bureau of Education, Bulletin No. 1, 1890), p. 9. Also National Education Association, *Proceedings,* 1889, pp. 291–99.

sioner of Education, commented favorably on the action of the two national organizations in 1881: [29]

> In Germany this degree is the reward purely of scholarship, which must be shown by examination and other tests; but in this country the value of the degree has been greatly impaired by the fact that many of the colleges confer it as an honorary doctorate. . . . So long as a few of our leading universities persist in this custom, it is not to be supposed that the smaller colleges will drop it.

He reported that 39 institutions had awarded the Ph.D. as an honorary degree from 1873 to 1889, and that the total number of such degrees in that period, 430, had varied from 15 to 50 each year.

Very important in continuing to focus attention of the academic world on the problem was the Federation of Graduate Clubs, representing the principal graduate schools of the country in the 1890's. At its meeting December 29, 1896, it passed the following resolution: [30]

> Resolved that it is the sense of this convention that it is inexpedient for any institutions to give the same degrees *honoris causa* as it grants in regular course on examination. . . . That the degrees of Ph.D., Sc.D., M.D., and Pd.D., should never be given *honoris causa* or *in absentia*. L.H.D., S.T.D., D.D., LL.D., D.C.L., and Mus.D. are recognized as honorary degrees.

A key figure in attempting to preserve the academic standing of the Ph.D. degree was Professor White of Harvard University. Addressing the annual meeting of the Federation of Graduate Clubs at Harvard in 1898, he said: [31]

> The fight should be waged unremittingly against the bad practice of conferring this degree *honoris causa*. In July 1881, I had the honor to propose a resolution on this subject to the American Philological Association in Cleveland, and was sent by it to lay the resolution before the American Association for the Advancement of Science. The resolution was adopted by both Associations, and a memorial was subsequently addressed to the governing boards of all American universities and colleges giving strong reasons why the degrees of Doctor of Philosophy and Doctor of Science should

---

[29] U. S. Commissioner of Education, *Annual Report,* 1889–90, p. 758.
[30] U. S. Commissioner of Education, *Annual Report,* 1896–97, pp. 1650–51.
[31] B. W. Barclay, University of Pennsylvania, ed., *Graduate Handbook No. 7* (Philadelphia, Pa.: J. B. Lippincott Co., 1899), p. 23.

not be conferred as honorary degrees. The document was signed by distinguished men. . . . The same protest has been renewed in many ways since that time, and the offenders are not so numerous, at least relatively, as they once were. The time has come, perhaps, for drastic measures. I propose to the Federation whether they should not publish each year, in their official organ, a blacklist of the offending colleges, preceded by an unequivocal statement of the nature of the offense.

This proposal apparently was not adopted by the Federation. It had been made earlier (1892) in an editorial by the influential *Educational Review,* then under the dynamic editorship of Nicholas Murray Butler: [32]

> This pernicious and demoralizing practice was more marked at the last commencement season than ever before. Scores of these degrees were given without any warrant whatever . . . . The suggestion has been made that the *Educational Review* should make a list of the colleges that persist in this abuse and publish it from time to time. It might be more efficacious to print a list of the persons who receive and accept such a degree.

The *Review* began to follow this policy in 1893 and continued for more than a decade to publish names both of the institutions and of the recipients.

In 1893 another editorial declared that "only Rutgers College and Brown University, among institutions of first rank, have made the serious mistake of conferring the degree of Ph.D. *causa honoris.*" [33]

In 1897 it published a list of four institutions, including Dartmouth and Union, which had given the degree "in utter defiance of educational sentiment and conviction." [34]

In 1898 its list included only two institutions, Tufts College and, *mirabale dictu,* Central High School of Philadelphia.[35]

The last such list was published in 1906, and consisted of a single institution, Syracuse University.[36] The *Educational Review*'s campaign, supplemented by other influences, had had considerable effect. The supposed prestige of the honorary degree rapidly lessened in the face of such publicity. Nevertheless the conferring of honor-

---

[32] *Educational Review,* 4 (September, 1892), p. 208.
[33] *Ibid.,* 6 (September, 1893), pp. 200–1.
[34] *Ibid.,* 14 (June, 1897), pp. 190.
[35] *Ibid.,* 16 (September, 1898), p. 220.
[36] *Ibid.,* 32 (September, 1906), p. 216.

ary Ph.D.'s was to continue sporadically for thirty years longer and more than 60 such degrees were conferred after 1906, chiefly by smaller and widely scattered institutions.

One important result of the agitation fostered by the Federation of Graduate Clubs was the organization in 1900 of the Association of American Universities which established minimum standards for residence, examination, and dissertation for the Ph.D. degree. Most of the smaller institutions which had been conferring the Ph.D. as an "earned" degree could not begin to meet these reasonable minimum standards.

Even as late as 1912, however, the situation was still far from satisfactory. Numerous institutions reported the conferral of the earned Ph.D. upon examination when their facilities were quite inadequate to sponsor any substantial graduate work. Thus the Commissioner of Education reported in 1912: [37]

> Certain institutions confer the Ph.D. and other academic degrees for work done wholly or chiefly *in absentia* and report such degrees as conferred on examination. This practice is so clearly akin to granting outright honorary degrees as to make it difficult to determine in which class such degrees ought to be listed. Few of the following institutions, which report the conferring of the Ph.D. degree on examination in 1911–12, have resources or equipment which would lead one to expect them to grant this degree at all, much less grant it to five or more each year: Spring Hill College, 1; Ewing College, 5; Kansas City University, 2; New Windsor College, 1; Grove City College, 12; and Cumberland University, 1.

Grove City College was reported that year as having 14 professors and 215 students, all undergraduates. It had *given* (the word is used advisedly) 19 Ph.D. degrees (all reported to the Commissioner of Education as earned degrees) over the past three years.

And even as late as 1924, Rensselaer Polytechnic Institute, as a feature of its centennial celebration, conferred honorary Ph.D. degrees on the presidents of Yale University, Cornell University, University of Wisconsin, and Massachusetts Institute of Technology, evidently without protest from these educational leaders.[38]

---

[37] U. S. Commissioner of Education, *Annual Report,* 1912, Vol. 2, p. 248.

[38] *The Centennial Celebration of Rensselaer Polytechnic Institute, Troy, New York, October 3rd to 4th, 1924* (Troy, N.Y.: Board of Trustees of the Institute, 1925), p. 14. See also Palmer C. Ricketts, *History of Rensselaer Polytechnic Institute* (New York: J. Wiley and Sons, 1895), p. 248.

It is only since about 1920 or 1925 that the standards for the Ph.D. degree may be considered as being satisfactorily established and observed. Although even as late as 1960 there were significant differences between institutions conferring it as an earned degree, there were none so glaring as in the early years of the century.

Other honorary doctorates. The recommendation of the Federation of Graduate Clubs "that the degrees of Ph.D., Sc.D., M.D., and Pd.D. should never be given *honoris causa*" has been followed as far as the Ph.D. and M.D. are concerned, but not in the case of the Sc.D. and the Ped.D.

In 1960 the Sc.D. was given as an honorary degree by 221 institutions, as an earned degree by only eight. The Doctor of Pedagogy has been superseded entirely as an earned degree by the Doctor of Education which was granted by 77 institutions in 1960, and as an honorary degree by 22 institutions. The Ped.D., on the other hand, was reported as an honorary degree by 22 institutions, as an earned degree by none. It would seem that the newer Ed.D. has been going through the same vicissitudes which the Ph.D. experienced, although it is to be hoped that it will not require as long a period to establish itself exclusively as an earned doctorate. The Doctor of Pedagogy, on the other hand, could well be used exclusively as the accepted honorary doctorate in the field of education.

Honorary Doctorates for Women

It has been estimated that about one percent of the total number of honorary degrees conferred in the United States have been conferred on women.[39] R. A. Smith found that 130 American colleges had given 262 honorary doctorates to women between 1882 and 1932—18 of them in the nineteenth century—but he found no record of any honorary degree given to a woman before 1882. He found that the ages of the women so honored varied from 31 to 99 years.[40]

The youngest was Eva La Gallienne, the actress, who in 1930 (at the age of 31) was given an honorary Doctor of Humane Letters by Smith College and a Doctor of Literature by Russell Sage Col-

[39] Walter Crosby Eells, "Norms for Honorary Degrees in American Colleges and Universities," *Educational Record,* 38 (October, 1957), p. 379.

[40] Ray A. Smith, *Women Recipients of Honorary Degrees in the United States* (Master's thesis presented at New York University, 1935), 29 pp.

lege. She also received a Doctor of Literature from Brown University in 1933, and one from Mount Holyoke College in 1937. (In 1927, at the age of 28, she had been given an honorary Master of Arts by Tufts College.)

The oldest recipient was Emily Howland (1827–1929) who on October 28, 1926, at the age of 99, was given an honorary degree of Doctor of Literature by the University of the State of New York (State Education Department), the first woman to be so honored by that agency. Probably hers is a record for age, not only among women but among men as well.

Although the University of the State of New York conferred 127 honorary doctorates between 1792 and 1960, only two of these were awarded to women. One was Miss Howland; the other Mildred McAfee Horton, who received a L.H.D. October 26, 1951, two years after her retirement from the presidency of Wellesley College. Mrs. Horton also received L.H.D. degrees from four other institutions and LL.D. degrees from 17 others—perhaps the record number of honorary doctorates held by a woman.

CHAPTER VI

The Master's Degree

Every Schollar that giveth up in writing a *System,* or *Synopsis,* or summe of *Logick,* Naturall and Morall *Phylosophy, Arithmetick, Geometry,* and *Astronomy:* and is ready to defend his *Theses* or positions: withall skilled in the Originalls as abovesaid: and of godly life & conversation: and so approved by the Overseers and Master of the Colledge, at any publique *Act,* is fit to be dignified with his 2d Degree.

Laws of Harvard College, 1642 [1]

In the Middle Ages (see Chap. I), the master's degree was virtually synonymous with the doctor's degree, both signifying competence to teach. The earliest form, the Master of Arts *(Magister Artium),* was later abandoned in favor of the doctorate on the Continent, but in England the doctor's degree was abandoned while the master's degree was retained as the highest earned degree in the arts faculties. Thus it came about that the master's degree was provided for in the first statutes of Harvard (see above) while the doctor's degree was virtually unknown in America, except as an honorary degree, for more than two centuries.

The master's degree in America has passed through various stages during the three centuries that it has been in use. In 1899 a Harvard University professor said that there had been at least six different classes of Master's degrees in use at that University: (1) *honoris causa* (see Chap. I and p. 63), (2) *ad eundem* (see Chap. I), (3) *in cursu,* (4) with a professional degree, (5) with the degree of Ph.D., and (6) *pro meritis.* [2]

---

[1] *New England's First Fruits* (London: R.O. and G.D. for Henry Overton, 1643), p. 16, as reproduced by Samuel E. Morison, *The Founding of Harvard College* (Cambridge, Mass.: Harvard University Press, 1935), p. 436. Josiah Quincy, *History of Harvard University* (Cambridge, Mass: John Owen, 1840), Vol. 1, p. 517, gives a slightly different version with modernization of spelling, capitalization, and use of italics.

[2] John W. Wright in discussion of paper by Eleanor O. Brownell, "The Master's Degree: Is It Obsolete?" in Barclay W. Bradley, *The Graduate Handbook, No. 7. The Organ of the Federation of Graduate Clubs* (Philadelphia, Pa.: J. B. Lippincott Co., 1899), pp. 55–8.

Master's Degree *in Cursu*

The 1642 requirements for a master's degree at Harvard were taken seriously for a considerable time, although later they were so modified in practice as to become almost meaningless. At first, however, the Master of Arts was considered the normal goal and end of an academic career. Following the medieval tradition, it was considered necessary to spend seven years to secure a masterate. This degree was intended to represent the knowledge of the liberal arts appropriate to the education of a Christian gentleman in colonial New England.

Accordingly, many young men, especially those studying for the ministry (the chief purpose for the founding of Harvard), remained at the college for part or all of the three-year period intervening between the A.B. and M.A. degrees, "reading divinity" under the guidance of the president, and often teaching one or two classes as well. In the period 1649–56, 53 young men took their A.B. degrees and 35 their M.A. degrees at Harvard. Ten of the 35 resided at the College the entire period between their two degrees, 15 resided there one year or more; three less than one year; and only six had no period of formal residence.[3]

How long this type of earned master's degree continued to be awarded at Harvard is somewhat uncertain. Its early academic importance, however, is indicated in part by the fact that separate commencement exercises for bachelors and masters, usually on the morning and afternoon of the same day, were maintained at Harvard until the beginning of the nineteenth century.[4]

In 1734, almost a century after its organization, Harvard's laws were amended to include the following statement regarding candidates for the master's degree: [5]

> What Bachelor soever shall make a common place or synopsis of any of the arts or sciences, and publicly read the same in the

---

[3] Samuel E. Morison, *Harvard College in the Seventeenth Century* (Cambridge, Mass.: Harvard University Press, 1936), p. 70. The numbers given total 34 instead of 35, but these are the figures as Morison reports them. Probably the "six" should be "seven."

[4] Morison, *op. cit.*, p. 69.

[5] Benjamin Peirce, *A History of Harvard University From Its Foundation in the Year 1636 to the Period of the American Revolution* (Cambridge, Mass.: Brown, Shattuck and Company, 1833), Appendix, pp. 135–37.

College hall, in the third year after his 1st degree, and be ready to defend his theses, and is skilled in the original tongues, and continueth blameless, shall, after approbation at a public act, be capable of a second degree, viz., of Master of Arts.

The nature of the theses that the candidate was required to defend "at a public act" is suggested by the list of 19 titles which was published, with the names of their defenders, in 1743. The eight selected for listing below cover scientific as well as political and theological fields.[6]

1. Whether the Dissolution of Solids in Corrosive Liquors be performed by Attraction?
2. Whether Private Profit ought to be the chief End of Moral Actions?
3. Whether it is lawful to resist the Supream Magistrate, if the the Common Wealth cannot be otherwise preserved?
4. Whether all Animal Motion and Sensation be performed by the Motion of the Nerves?
5. Whether Justification be best discovered by Works attending Sanctification?
6. Whether every Form of Divine Worship, may be universally tolerated, in no manner incommoding the public good?
7. Whether the Scripture be the perfect and only Rule of Believing and Acting?
8. Whether the Law of Nation be distinct from the Law of Nature?

It is worthy of note that the third entry was affirmed by the youthful Samuel Adams, who was later to take a leading part in resisting the British rule in order to preserve the Commonwealth of Massachusetts and the associated American colonies.

The Harvard laws of 1734 contain further interesting provisions —financial and gastronomic as well as academic—to assure that the candidate in his conduct had "continued blameless"; evidently to guard against unseemly practices that had developed: [7]

Each candidate for his first or second degree shall pay twenty shillings to the President and twenty shillings to the Steward toward defraying the charge of the Commencement dinner; and each candidate for his second degree shall pay twenty shillings to the Steward for the use of the College. . . . For preventing disorder and extravagances at Commencement, it is ordered. . . . That a dinner

---

[6] *Ibid.*, Appendix, iii.
[7] *Ibid.*, Appendix, pp. 135–37.

be provided in the hall as usual. And that no commencer shall have
at his chamber any plumb cake, or plain cake, or pyee, or hot meats
of any sort, except what is left of the dinner in the hall; or any
brandy, rum, or any distilled spirits or composition made with any
of them. And if any of these prohibited drinks or provisions shall
be found in the chambers or studies of any of the commencers, or
within any of the dependencies thereof, such defender shall be liable
to be debarred his degrees. And whosoever, after he has taken his
degree, shall, at that Commencement, act contrary to any of these
prohibitions, and be convicted thereof within three months, shall
be liable to be denied his second degree, if a Bachelor; and if a
Master, he shall be liable to be denied a diploma, and all privilege
of ever living at the College; and the Corporation with the Tutors
shall visit the chambers of the commencers to see that this law be
well observed.

The first degree of Master of Arts at Yale was awarded in 1702,
upon examination, to Nathaniel Chauncey who was given an A.B.
degree the same year.[8]
How long full insistence upon the stated academic requirements
for the master's degree continued is uncertain. Probably the change
was gradual. As early as 1759 Princeton tried to restore some of its
waning significance by stating that when master's degrees "are pro-
miscuously distributed as cursory Formalities after the usual Interval
of Time without any previous Evidence of suitable Qualifications,
they sink into Contempt as insignificant Ceremonies," and that
therefore candidates for the master's degrees would be required to
reside in college for *one week* before Commencement and stand examinations in the branches directly connected with "that Profession
of life which they have entered upon or have in view." [9]
By the early nineteenth century the master's degree had ceased to
have much scholarly significance. The master's degree *in cursu* came
to be referred to humorously by students as the master's degree "of
course." Its requirements in practice were summarized in student
language as "keeping out of jail for three years and paying the five-

---

[8] "He had resided for a short time before Commencement with Rector Pierson,
and presented himself to the Corporation as a candidate for the degree of B.A.;
but being found upon examination to be worthy of the higher degree, he was
advanced at once to the grade of M.A." From Franklin B. Dexter, *Biographical
Sketches of the Graduates of Yale College, with Annals of the College History,
October 1701–May 1745* (New York: Henry Holt & Co., 1885), pp. 9–10.

[9] Varnum Lansing Collins, *Princeton* (New York: Oxford University Press,
1914), p. 55.

dollar fee." Yet the tradition of a seven-year course for a fully educated man was strong enough to make the majority of Harvard graduates continue to take their second degree even though its earlier scholarly significance had almost completely disappeared.

This purely formal use of the Master of Arts *in cursu* continued in most American Colleges and universities for the first three quarters of the nineteenth century, although a few Southern institutions seem not to have followed the general practice. The 1870's marked a general transition from the award of the degree *in cursu* to *pro meritis*.

In his statement for the use of foreign ambassadors and ministers (see p. 7), Commissioner Eaton in 1877 wrote: [10]

> Usually a degree in course called the Master of Arts (A.M.) is conferred three years after graduation on bachelors of arts who are engaged in literary or professional pursuits and who pay to their college a fee prescribed by its regulations. There are exceptions to this rule. The University of Virginia never gave this degree except to persons studying and passing examinations in certain specified branches. Harvard, Yale, and some other colleges have discontinued the practice.

The M.A. *in cursu* was conferred upon thousands of graduates of American colleges prior to 1870, but no record of the actual number has ever been made. In some institutions, too, it is difficult to distinguish between this type of master's degree, and those reported as purely honorary degrees.

Master's Degree *pro Meritis*

In the latter part of the nineteenth century, with the new and expanding standards for graduate education, the need for rehabilitating the discredited master's degree programs was felt by various leading institutions of higher education.

The University of Michigan appears to have been the first major university to provide for the new or rehabilitated master's degree. Its catalogue for 1853 announced "that the degree of Master of Arts would not be conferred in course upon graduates of three years' standing, but only upon such graduates as had pursued professional or general scientific studies during that period. The candidate for the degree must also pass an examination and read a thesis before

[10] U. S. Commissioner of Education, *Annual Report*, 1877, p. cvii.

the Faculty at the time of taking the degree." [11] Evidently this announcement was premature, for the university historian states: "But the word of promise that was now spoken to the ear was broken to the hope." The catalogue announcement of 1853 remained a dead letter until December 1858 when the Regents of the University provided for a change in the requisites for conferring the degree of Master of Arts and for the adoption of the Master of Science. The requirements included taking at least two courses each semester for one year, passing an examination, and presenting a thesis to the faculty. One such degree was conferred in 1859. Unfortunately, however, the old type of master's degree *in cursu* was also continued, and was not dropped until 1877. "This time," the historian observed happily, "the promise was kept to the hope as well as spoken to the ear." [12]

The University of North Carolina was only a year later than Michigan in making a similar announcement. The first earned degree of the new type, with a thesis, was granted in 1856, but the practice was abandoned before 1860.[13]

At the University of Georgia the old practice was continued until 1868, when a course of study was required for the M.S. degree. The first award of the new type was made in 1871.[14]

At Harvard University, with the accession of President Charles W. Eliot in 1869, the old type of master's degree was promptly abolished, and since that date only the new type has been awarded.

Harvard's example was followed by Yale University and the University of Pennsylvania in 1876, by Princeton in 1879, and by Columbia in 1881. Many smaller institutions followed the example of these leaders. But in many cases for the 1870's it is difficult or impossible to tell from published statistics which were the old type and which the new type of master's degrees. Dartmouth, however, did not abandon the old type until 1893 and conferred its first Master of Arts on examination in 1896.

Thus, the modern type of earned master's degrees, involving significant work on the graduate level, came into general acceptance

---

[11] Burke A. Hinsdale, *History of the University of Michigan* (Ann Arbor, Mich.: The University, 1906), p. 88.

[12] *Ibid.*, p. 89.

[13] Walton C. John, *Graduate Study in Colleges and Universities in the United States* (Washington, D.C.: U.S. Department of the Interior: Office of Education, 1935; Bulletin 1934, No. 20), pp. 8–9.

[14] *Ibid.*, p. 9.

in the latter part of the nineteenth century and is the characteristic type, with some variations among different institutions and at different periods, during the twentieth century.

Other Master's Degrees

The only master's degree awarded during the greater part of the first two centuries of American collegiate history was the classic Master of Arts. The Master of Science was provided for at the University of Michigan as early as 1858. It was authorized by other institutions soon after they provided for the Bachelor of Science degree (see Chap. VII).

In 1960, 322 institutions reported that they were offering the M.A. without qualification, and 253 institutions the M.S. In addition to these unqualified degrees, however, no fewer than 121 varieties of Master of Arts were offered—from Master of Arts in Anthropology to Master of Arts in Urban Planning—and 272 varieties of the Master of Science—from Master of Science in Aeronautical Engineering to Master of Science in Zoology.[15]

The comparatively recent Master of Education was offered by 177 institutions, and the Master of Business Administration by 111. Eleven other master's degrees, most of them originating in the twentieth century and reported as offered in 1960 by 25 or more institutions, follow in order of frequency: Master of Music, Master of Fine Arts, Master of Arts in Education, Master of Religious Education, Master of Science in Electrical Engineering, Master of Science in Civil Engineering, Master of Theology, Master of Music Education, Master of Sacred Theology, Master of Law, and Master of Social Work. Most of these require only one year of graduate work, but for a few two years are required, at least in some institutions.

Number of Master's Degrees Awarded

The number of *pro meritis* or earned master's degrees awarded from 1870 to 1960 is reported as approximately 1,300,000, 34 per-

---

[15] See Walter Crosby Eells and Harold A. Haswell, *Academic Degrees: Earned and Honorary Degrees Conferred by Institutions of Higher Education in the United States* (Washington, D.C.: U.S. Department of Health, Education, and Welfare: Office of Education, 1961), pp. 248–69, for lists of these and frequency of their use.

cent of which were awarded to women. For the period 1951–60 the average number has been almost 64,000 per year. During the same period the number of baccalaureate and other first-level degrees has averaged almost 340,000 per year. Thus the number of master's degrees conferred annually is almost one-fifth (19 percent) of the number of baccalaureate degrees. This indicates a very high proportion of students completing at least one year of graduate work. In 1900 the corresponding figure was less than six percent.[16]

Increasingly, although perhaps undesirably, the master's degree is becoming the characteristic degree among college and university teachers. In 1953–54, in a study of 59,000 faculty members in over 600 colleges, the National Education Association found that 49 percent held the master's degree but no higher degrees. But in 1960–61, of over 11,000 new college teachers, 57 percent had master's degrees only.[17] The same study showed doctor's degrees were held by 40 percent of college teachers in 1953–54, but by only 26 percent of new college teachers in 1960–61. To some extent, therefore, the shortage of holders of the doctorate for college teaching positions (which seems certain to become more acute before 1970) is being taken up by men and women with the master's degree only.

Master's degrees for women. The number of master's degrees earned by women has increased from only 300 in 1900 to 23,560 in 1960. The proportion, however, has decreased markedly in recent years, from almost 40 percent in 1930 and 1940 to less than 32 percent in 1960 as shown by the following summary:

NUMBER OF MASTER'S DEGREES

Year	Total	Women	Percent Women
1900	1,583	303	19.1%
1910	2,113	558	26.4
1920	4,279	1,294	30.2
1930	14,629	5,791	39.6
1940	26,731	10,223	38.2
1950	58,216	16,982	29.2
1960	74,497	23,560	31.6

16 *Earned Degrees Conferred, 1958–1959* (Washington, D.C.: U.S. Department of Health, Education, and Welfare: Office of Education, Circular No. 636, 1961), p. 16.

17 *Teacher Supply and Demand in Universities, Colleges, and Junior Colleges, 1959–60 and 1960–61* (Washington, D.C.: Research Division, National Education Association, May 1961), p. 13.

Problems Connected with Master's Degrees

Various problems regarding the true function and possible modifications in the requirements for the master's degree and the best uses of it have been under discussion at intervals during the twentieth century. Should the master's degree be regarded as a terminal degree, significant in itself? If so, for what purposes or positions? Chiefly for secondary-school teachers, or for college teachers? Should it be concerned with subject matter or should it include pedagogical methodology? Should it be thought of merely as a stepping stone on the way to the doctorate? Should the period of study for it be increased to two years? Should a thesis or dissertation be required? These and related questions have been the subject of debate for almost a century, and no general agreement has been reached on most of them.

The reports of the Committee on Graduate Policies in Education of the Association of Graduate Schools, especially at their annual meetings in 1957, 1958, and 1959 made vigorous recommendations for "revitalizing the master's degree." [18] These were only the latest of a series of committee reports dealing with various phases of the problem. [19]

[18] Association of Graduate Schools in the Association of American Universities, *Proceedings*, 1957, pp. 33–48; 1958, pp. 31–49; 1959, pp. 36–43.

[19] "The Master's Degrees," Association of American Universities, *Proceedings*, 1945, 46th Annual Meeting, pp. 108–37. This important report of the Committee on Graduate Work and Teacher Training, under the chairmanship of Dean R.G.D. Richardson of Brown University, refers to earlier reports to the Association on the same subject made in 1935, 1936, and 1939. The purpose of the 1945 committee was "to formulate an ideal for the M.A. and the M.S. and for some of the professional Master's degrees." The Committee's report was followed by a 12-page discussion of its recommendations. The report a decade later of the Committee on Policies in Graduate Education (Association of Graduate Schools in the Association of American Universities, *Proceedings*, 1955, pp. 11–47), under the chairmanship of Dean Leonard B. Beach of Vanderbilt University, while devoted chiefly to the Ph.D. degree, contained an important section on the master's degree. See also "Requirements for the Master's Degree," *AAUP Bulletin*, 18 (March, 1932), pp. 169–85. This report of Committee M of the American Association of University Professors (Tucker Brooke, Yale, Chairman) gives the judgments of many individuals on nine important questions, including proper length of course, final examination, thesis requirements, and foreign language requirements. For a critical review of significant publications, see William W. Brickman, "The Master of Arts and the Ph.D.," *School and Society*, 66 (August 30, 1947), pp. 169–74.

Honorary Master's Degrees

In earlier years the master's degree was given with considerable frequency as an honorary degree, but except for the special type of *privatim* degrees (see Chap. I), their use for this purpose has decreased markedly in recent years.

In 1875 the Commissioner of Education reported 130 honorary M.A. degrees out of a total of 398 honorary degrees conferred that year, or 35 percent.[20] Professor Smith reports 904 honorary master's degrees 1880 to 1886, or an average of 151 per year.[21] In 1912, the U. S. Commissioner of Education said: [22]

> While the great majority of these degrees are almost universally recognized as honorary, like D.D. and LL.D., it is still unfortunately common to find A.M., M.S., and B.S. conferred in considerable number as honorary degrees.

In 1916 the Commissioner reported 165 master's degrees out of a total of 877 honorary degrees conferred that year. Of these, 122 were M.A., 18 were M.S., and 25 were ten other types of master's degrees.[23] R. A. Smith found that of the 344 honorary degrees conferred on women between 1882 and 1932, 82, or 24 percent, were master's degrees.[24]

In 1960, 34 institutions reported that they had conferred the Master of Arts and 21 the Master of Science as honorary degrees "in recent years." In addition, 22 other honorary masterates were reported conferred by smaller numbers of institutions (the Master of Letters by four, and the Master of Education by three). At least 32 other honorary master's degrees have been conferred in past years but are no longer current.

One of the first honorary M.A. degrees given in America was conferred on Benjamin Franklin in July 1753 by Harvard University. He also received one in September 1753 at Yale University; and one in April 1756 at the College of William and Mary. It is

---

20 U.S. Commissioner of Education, *Annual Report*, 1875, p. xcix, pp. 782–90.

21 Charles Forster Smith, *Honorary Degrees Conferred in American Colleges* (Washington, D.C.: U.S. Bureau of Education, Bulletin No. 1, 1890), p. 7.

22 U.S. Commissioner of Education, *Annual Report*, 1912, p. 248.

23 U.S. Commissioner of Education, *Annual Report*, 1916, Vol. II, p. 251.

24 Ray A. Smith, *Women Recipients of Honorary Degrees in the United States* (Master's thesis presented at New York University, 1935), 29 pp.

rather strange that Franklin himself, in his famed *Autobiography*, confused the order of these degrees: [25]

> The business of the Post-Office occasion'd my taking a Journey this Year [1753] to New England, where the College of Cambridge of their own Motion, presented me with the degree of Master of Arts. Yale College, in Connecticut, had before made me a similar compliment. Thus without studying in any College, I came to partake of their Honours. They were confer'd in Consideration of my Improvements and Discoveries in the electric Branch of Natural Philosophy.

This error has been reproduced uncritically in many later works concerning Franklin. It is a little surprising that even after he achieved greater fame as a diplomat, statesman, and philosopher, he never received the higher honor of the doctorate from any American institution, although he did receive such honors from the University of St. Andrews in 1759 and from the University of Oxford in 1762. A dozen other errors regarding the honorary degrees which he did receive are found in the published literature, some of them in very recent years.[26]

---

[25] Max Farrand, *Benjamin Franklin's Memoirs: Parallel Text Edition* (Berkeley and Los Angeles: University of California Press, 1949), p. 324.

[26] Walter Crosby Eells, "Benjamin Franklin's Honorary Degrees," *College and University*, 37 (Fall, 1961), pp. 5–26.

CHAPTER VII

The Bachelor's Degree

> Every Schollar, that on proofe is found able to read the Originalls of the *Old* and *New Testament* into the Latine tongue, and to resolve them *Logically;* withall being of godly life and conversation; And at any publick Act hath the Approbation of the Overseers and Master of the Colledge, is fit to be dignified with his first Degree.
>
> *Laws of Harvard College*, 1642 [1]

To this statement of the first requirements for a "first degree" at Harvard College, published in *New England's First Fruits* in 1643, the "Lawes, Liberties, and orders of Harvard Colledge confirmed by the Overseers and president of the Colledge in the Yeares 1642, 1643, 1644, 1645, and 1646, and published to the Scholars for the perpetuall preservation of their welfare and government," adds the following: "viz., Bachelor of Arts: otherwise no scholar may be admitted to a first degree, unless he hath been at the Colledge three years and ten months at the least, from his admission being blameless and having attended upon and performed all public exercises." [2]

Early Baccalaureate Degrees

In Europe, the bachelor's degree came into use much later than the doctor's or master's degree. The term first appeared at the University of Paris in the thirteenth century,[3] where it was used to designate not the completion of a systematic course of study, but its beginning: it marked entrance to an apprenticeship status preparatory to the master's degree.

The word *bachelor*, according to the *Oxford English Dictionary*,

---

[1] *New England's First Fruits* (London, 1643), p. 16, as reproduced by Samuel E. Morison, *The Founding of Harvard College* (Cambridge, Mass.: Harvard University Press, 1935), p. 436.

[2] Benjamin Peirce, *A History of Harvard University From Its Foundation in the Year 1636 to the Period of the American Revolution* (Cambridge, Mass.: Brown, Shattuck and Company, 1833), Appendix, pp. 135–37.

[3] Henry B. Green, "The Origin of the A.B. Degree," *Journal of Higher Education*, 17 (April, 1946), pp. 205–10.

is of doubtful origin, but probably derived from the Latin *bacca* or *vacca*, a cow; and a *baccalarius* or *baccalaureus* was one who was engaged in the care of cows. The transition from cowherd, to peasant, to young man without a specific occupation, to young man as an apprentice, is involved but logical. *Baccalaureus* has often been identified with *bacca* and *lauri*, the laurel berry, whence laurel wreath and poet laureate as marks of distinction, but the *Oxford English Dictionary* dismisses this as erroneous.

The first historian of Harvard, Cotton Mather, gives quite a different derivation, which has historical interest although no recognized philological validity. Regarding the early Commencement exercises at Harvard he wrote: [4]

> These exercises were, besides an oration usually made by the President, orations both *Salutatory* and *Valedictory* made by some or other of the commencers, . . . and these orations were made not only in Latin, but sometimes in Greek and in Hebrew also; and some of them were in verse, and even in Greek verse, as well as others in prose. But the main exercises were *disputations* upon questions, wherein the *respondents* first made their theses; for according to Vossius, the very essence of the BACCALAUREUS being but a name corrupted of *Batualius,* which *Batualius* (as well as the French Bataile) comes *a Batuendo,* a business that carries *beating* in it: . . . they were called *Battailers* because they had battled as it were with an antagonist—that is, had engaged in a public controversy or discussion, and thus given a specimen of their proficiency.

Chaucer in 1386 speaks of a "Bacheler of Lawe." The term was in common use in the English universities in the sixteenth century, and was thus adopted by the American colonies.

In America, the bachelor's degree was first conferred in 1642 on nine young men who made up the first graduating class of Harvard College. Table 2 shows its first use in 18 other institutions which granted it in the seventeenth and eighteenth centuries and the total number conferred before 1801. Of the 9,144 baccalaureate degrees reported in Table 2, all were the Bachelor of Arts except for 149 Bachelor of Medicine (or Bachelor of Physic) degrees at Harvard, Columbia, Pennsylvania, Rutgers, and Dartmouth; and one Bach-

---

[4] Cotton Mather, "The History of Harvard College," in *Old South Leaflets* (Boston, Mass.: Directors of the Old South Work, Old South Meeting House, n.d.), Vol. VIII, No. 184, p. 8.

elor of Law at William and Mary. Of the total, 4,773, or slightly over half, were conferred before the Declaration of Independence by the nine colonial colleges chartered before 1776.[5]

TABLE 2

COLLEGES CONFERRING BACCALAUREATE DEGREES, 1642–1800

Institution	Charter Year	Year	Number	Total before 1801
Harvard University	1636[a]	1642	9	3,544
(Harvard College)				
College of William and Mary	1693	1700 ?	?	30
Yale University	1701	1702	1	2,339
(Yale College)				
Princeton University	1746	1748	6	917
(College of New Jersey)				
Columbia University	1754	1758	7	328
(King's College)				
University of Pennsylvania	1755	1756	6	460
(College, Academy, and Charitable School of Philadelphia)				
Brown University	1765	1769	7	345
(College of Rhode Island)				
Rutgers University	1766	1774	1	68
(Queen's College)				
Dartmouth College	1769	1771	4	654
Washington College (Md.)	1782	1783	8	53
Washington and Lee University	1782	1785	12	19
(Liberty Hall Academy)				
Hampden-Sydney College	1783	1786	8	35
Dickinson College	1783	1787	9	166
St. John's College	1784	1793	3	31
College of Charleston	1785	1794	6	6
University of North Carolina	1789	1798	7	19
Williams College	1793	1795	4	94
Union College and University	1795	1797	3	30
(Union College)				
Washington College (Tenn.)	1795	1796	2	6
				9,144

[a] Established by vote of General Court of Colony of Massachusetts Bay; first charter, 1650.

Source: Walter Crosby Eells, *Baccalaureate Degrees Conferred by American Colleges in the 17th and 18th Centuries* (Washington, D.C.: U.S. Department of Health, Education, and Welfare: Office of Education, Circular No. 528, May 1958), pp. 4–10.

[5] Walter Crosby Eells, *Baccalaureate Degrees Conferred by American Colleges in the 17th and 18th Centuries* (Washington, D.C.: U.S. Department of Health, Education, and Welfare: Office of Education, Circular No. 528, May 1958), pp. 4–10, 20, 26.

The first Bachelor of Arts was conferred by Harvard in 1642; the first Bachelor of Medicine (or Physic) by Pennsylvania in 1768; the first Bachelor of Law by the College of William and Mary in 1793. These three baccalaureate degrees appear to be the only ones that were used by American institutions in the seventeenth and eighteenth centuries.

Later Baccalaureate Degrees

Except in the field of medicine, there was little need for any first degree other than the B.A. until well into the nineteenth century. Harvard and other colonial institutions had attempted by a single almost rigid curriculum to give the essentials of a *liberal* education to the young men who entered them. "Liberal education" at that time comprised chiefly a continuation of the *trivium* (grammar, rhetoric, and logic) and *quadrivium* (arithmetic, geometry, astronomy, and music) of the Middle Ages—the seven liberal *arts*. It may be noted that these "arts" included mathematics and science as well as the humanities, hence the Bachelor of *Arts* was sufficiently inclusive to cover them all. The development of marked differentiation among college curricula, and the introduction of other sciences, which began about the middle of the nineteenth century, altered the significance of the B.A. In many institutions it came to signify a major emphasis on the classics and in some institutions it came to be deemed inappropriate for men who were doing their chief work in the newly developing fields of science. Hence a more appropriate and distinctive degree was adopted: the Bachelor of Science. And with the development of specialized schools of theology, law, and engineering, professional degrees, Bachelor of Theology, Bachelor of Law, and various engineering degrees came into use.

The Bachelor of Science degree was conferred on four men at Harvard University who in 1851 completed their work in the recently organized (1847) Lawrence Scientific School of the University. It was the first use of this degree at Harvard. Rensselaer Polytechnic Institute, in its charter was given the power specifically to confer the Bachelor of Science degree (see p. 9). In practice, however, it conferred the more specialized form of Bachelor of Natural Science (B.N.S.) from 1835 to 1849. The Institute conferred its first degree of Bachelor of Science in 1850 (on Jose Tell Ferrao, who before 1860 became principal of a school for young ladies in Brazil). As far as the writer has been able to determine, this was the first use of the B.S. degree in the United States.[6]

The proliferation of baccalaureate degrees continued apace in the latter half of the nineteenth and in the twentieth centuries, although none of the newer degrees has begun to approach the popularity of the A.B. and B.S. In 1960 the Bachelor of Arts was reported conferred by 1,005 institutions, including practically all the liberal arts colleges and many of the universities and state colleges. Second in frequency was the B.S., reported as conferred by 779 institutions.

Other baccalaureate degrees conferred by 100 or more institutions in 1960 include (in order of frequency): Bachelor of Science in Education, Bachelor of Music, Bachelor of Science in Music, Bachelor of Science in Business Administration, Bachelor of Divinity, Bachelor of Science in Home Economics, and Bachelor of Science in Electrical Engineering. A total of almost 700 kinds of baccalaureate degrees (including at least 426 specialized B.S. degrees, 108 specialized B.A. degrees, 27 varieties of Bachelor of Music degrees and 29 varieties of Bachelor of Fine Arts degrees) were reported in current use in 1960.[7]

At the same time that this excessive multiplication of baccalaureate degrees was in progress, a contrary trend was developing—chiefly in the liberal arts colleges: a return to the single, all-inclusive B.A. In 1901, the Commissioner of Education wrote: [8]

---

[6] Early records of Rensselaer were destroyed by fire. The earliest extant record is a list of graduates published in the institution's *Annual Register* for 1860. A photographic copy of p. 31 of this publication, kindly furnished by John A. Dunlop, Registrar, December 18, 1961, shows that Mr. Ferrao received the B.S. degree in 1850. That little, if any, distinction was made between the B.S. and B.N.S. degrees is indicated by the fact that Henry B. Nason's *Biographical Record of the Officers and Graduates of the Rensselaer Polytechnic Institute 1824–1886* (Troy, N.Y.: William H. Young, 1889), reports Mr. Ferrao with the B.S. degree on p. 117, but with the B.N.S. degree on p. 281. Palmer C. Ricketts, *History of the Rensselaer Polytechnic Institute, 1824–1894* (New York: John Wiley & Sons, 1895), p. 178, reports Ferrao as receiving the B.S. degree.

[7] Walter Crosby Eells and Harold A. Haswell, *Academic Degrees: Earned and Honorary Degrees Conferred by Institutions of Higher Education in the United States* (Washington, D.C.: U.S. Department of Health, Education, and Welfare: Office of Education, 1960), pp. 207–33.

[8] U. S. Commissioner of Education, *Annual Report*, 1901, p. 1613. See also W. S. Sutton, "Unification of College Degrees," *School Review*, 8 (February, 1900), pp. 92–123, which gives the judgments of many college presidents and other educators of the period on giving both the A.B. and B.S. degrees.

There seems to be a tendency among the institutions of higher education toward adopting the single degree of Bachelor of Arts as representing a general liberal college culture. This degree can no longer be accepted as representing only a classical education, as it is the only degree now conferred by 137 institutions on the completion of what are known as liberal in contradistinction to technical courses of study. The dropping of the Ph.B., B.L., and B.S. degrees has been going on for some time.

Although the Commissioner correctly remarked the tendency to drop the degrees of Bachelor of Philosophy and Bachelor of Literature (in 1960 only 12 institutions reported the use of the former degree and only four the latter) he could scarcely have been more mistaken regarding the Bachelor of Science which is now offered by almost 800 institutions in more than 400 specialized forms. Of 745 liberal arts colleges which were offering bachelor's degrees in 1960, only 115 reported that they were conferring the Bachelor of Arts only, and some of these had never conferred any other baccalaureate degree. This is a considerable reduction in the number and proportion reported by the Commissioner of Education in 1901.

At least two major efforts have been made in the present century to change the length of time required to secure the bachelor's degree. President Nicholas Murray Butler of Columbia University, in his annual report for 1901–1902, proposed that the practice be changed so as to give the A.B. at the end of two years and the A.M. two years later.[9] A similar suggestion had been made a decade earlier by Charles K. Adams [10] and by President Gilman of Johns Hopkins University.[11]

President Butler's proposal was extensively discussed in academic circles and articles concerning it were published in the influential *Educational Review* by President Eliot of Harvard, President Harper of Chicago, and others, but nothing came of the proposal.

A more serious effort along the same line was put into practice a half century later at the University of Chicago under the presidency of Robert M. Hutchins. He proposed to award the A.B. degree at the close of a new four-year college course comprising the

---

[9] Edward C. Elliott, *The Rise of a University* (New York: Columbia University Press, 1937), Vol. II, pp. 211–12.

[10] Charles K. Adams, "The Next Step in Education," *Forum*, 10 (February, 1891), pp. 629–30.

[11] Daniel C. Gilman, "The Shortening of the College Curriculum," *Educational Review*, 1 (January, 1891), p. 107.

last two years of the typical high school curriculum and the first two years of the standard college, that is at the end of the conventional sophomore year. This proposal was widely discussed and vigorously attacked at various educational meetings, especially of the American Council on Education. Educators characterized the proposal as unnecessary, undesirable, and unfortunate and as a "counterfeit bachelor's degree." [12] In spite of extensive opposition to the plan, the University of Chicago adopted it in 1942 and the new type of abbreviated bachelor's degree was conferred on numerous students for the next five years. After President Hutchins left the University, the plan was abolished, but an occasional A.B. of this type was still awarded as late as 1961 to students who had entered under the Hutchins plan.

The need for an academic degree at the sophomore level appears to be fully met, both in junior colleges and in universities, by the associate's degree (see Chap. VIII).

An interesting although quite nonsignificant use of the bachelor's degree may be noted in the case of Central High School, Philadelphia. This school, under a special charter granted in 1849, has for more than a century conferred both the A.B. and the B.S. on its graduates. These degrees are recognized only as marking high school graduation—a harmless conceit from the past. The school—whose administrative head is known as the president, not the principal—has even conferred an honorary Ph.D. (see p. 68).[13]

Baccalaureate Degrees for Women

It was not until more than two hundred years after the first baccalaureate degrees were earned by men in America that the first ones were awarded to women.

Wesleyan College, Georgia (chartered 1836), then known as Georgia Female College, claims the distinction of having the first graduates from a chartered college for women (its first class of 11 young women was graduated in 1840). While the diplomas at that time were referred to only as a "First Degree," these and the later

---

[12] See Walter Crosby Eells, *Associate's Degree and Graduation Practices in Junior Colleges* (Washington, D.C.: American Association of Junior Colleges, 1942), pp. 78–82, for an annotated bibliography of 31 books and other publications on the subject.

[13] Personal letter from William M. Duncan, Associate Superintendent in charge of Secondary Schools, Philadelphia, November 7, 1961.

"Second Degrees" were listed in catalogs of later years as A.B. and A.M. degrees. The diploma of the first graduate modestly claims that Miss Catherine E. Brewer had "passed through the regular Course of Study . . . embracing all the sciences which are usually taught in the colleges of the United States, with such as appropriately belongs to Female Education in its most ample range." [14]

Although Wesleyan was the first college to confer baccalaureate degrees on women, the first college to admit young women on the same basis as men was Oberlin College, founded in 1833. In 1841 it graduated a class of nine men and three women—the first women to receive a Bachelor of Arts degree, but not the first to receive a baccalaureate degree.

In the nineteenth century, there was much doubt as to the propriety of young women receiving a "bachelor's" degree at all. The word *bachelor* had two rather distinct meanings—one denoting marital status, the other, academic status. Hence the incongruity in the minds of many collegiate educators of giving young women "bachelor's" degrees.

Various substitutes were suggested and adopted. In 1882 the Commissioner of Education reported the use of such designations for women's degrees as Licentiate of Instruction, Laureate of Science, Graduate in Liberal Arts, Proficient in Music.[15] In addition to these neutral terms, more distinctively feminine ones, such as Mistress of Arts, Maid of Philosophy, or Sister of Arts, were found. The "Mistress" series proved the most popular and soon extended into such specialized fields as Mistress of Art, Mistress of Classical Literature, Mistress of English, Mistress of English Literature, Mistress of Liberal Arts, Mistress of Liberal Learning, Mistress of Music, Mistress of Philosophy, Mistress of Polite Literature, and Mistress of Teaching. The Maid of Arts degree was conferred in several Southern states, the Maid of English and the Maid of Science were used in the West. Sister of Arts was awarded by Wheaton College, Illinois, from 1873 to 1876. In 1888 Bryce, in his *American Commonwealth*, commented on the Mistress of Polite Literature, Mistress of Music, and Maid of Philosophy.[16]

---

[14] Copy supplied by Ruth H. Young, Librarian, Wesleyan College, January 12, 1960.

[15] U. S. Commissioner of Education, *Annual Report*, 1882, p. 263.

[16] James Bryce, *The American Commonwealth* (London: Macmillan, 1888) p. 538.

When these distinctively feminine degrees of baccalaureate level were first used is not definitely known, but Beaver College, Pennsylvania, a college for women established in 1853, reports that its first two graduates in 1856 received degrees of Mistress of Liberal Arts and Mistress of English Literature. "Mistress" degrees had been authorized, however, more than twenty years earlier, although available records do not show that they were actually conferred. In 1835 the Legislature of Kentucky granted a charter to Van Doren's College for Young Ladies, with power to confer degrees of Mistress of Polite Literature, Mistress of Music, and Mistress of Instruction. But the college closed before 1839, and there is no record of its having used this power.

In 1872 the Commissioner of Education reported 39 degrees conferred by "Institutions for the Superior Instruction of Women": Mistress of English Literature, 15; Mistress of Arts, 13; Mistress of Liberal Arts, seven; Mistress of Music, three; and Mistress of Philosophy, one. In 1885–86, the number had increased: the Mistress of Arts was awarded to 180 graduates in 26 institutions; the Mistress of English Literature to 75 graduates in 16 institutions; the Mistress of Music to 16 graduates in six institutions; and the Mistress of Liberal Arts to 12 graduates in four institutions.

After 1886 the Commissioner reported only the number of graduates from colleges for women without indicating the different degrees given. It is probable that the number of "Mistresses" and other distinctively feminine degrees declined in the last decade of the nineteenth century. That they did not cease, however, for at least another quarter century is indicated by the fact that the catalogue of Burritt College, Tennessee, for 1924 announced the degrees of Bachelor of Arts and Bachelor of Science for young men, but Mistress of Arts and Mistress of Science for young women. The college closed in 1924 or 1925.

During the greater part of the twentieth century most institutions have made no distinction between degrees for men and for women, except as a matter of natural selection due to subject matter studied, and even here there is no sharp line of demarcation. Thus in 1959–60, women received 145 baccalaureate degrees in engineering, and three in military science; while men were awarded 81 degrees in nursing and 60 in home economics.

The number of baccalaureate (and first professional) bachelor's degrees earned by women has increased from some 5,000 in 1900 to almost 140,000 in 1960, but the proportion has decreased in recent years (although showing an increase in 1960 over 1950) as indicated by U.S. Office of Education reports:

NUMBER OF BACCALAUREATE DEGREES

Year	Total	Women	Percent Women *
1900	27,410	5,237	19.1
1910	37,199	8,437	22.7
1920	48,622	16,642	34.2
1930	122,484	48,869	39.9
1940	186,500	76,954	41.3
1950	432,058	103,217	23.9
1960	394,889	139,385	35.3

* The percentage pattern has followed the general pattern already tabulated for the Master's degree (see p. 9).

Total Number of Baccalaureate Degrees

The total number of baccalaureate degrees conferred from 1642 to 1961 has been estimated as 10,500,000.[17] Thirty-six institutions had conferred more than 50,000 earned degrees each, before 1960—for a total of 3,517,000. The great majority of these were baccalaureate degrees. Twenty-one publicly controlled institutions awarded 1,958,000 degrees; 15 privately controlled institutions awarded 1,559,000 degrees. The University of California was credited with the largest number—258,000—followed closely by Columbia University—251,000. These were the only two institutions which conferred more than 200,000 degrees each. The leading college for women was Hunter College, New York, which awarded nearly 50,000 degrees.[18]

Honorary Baccalaureate Degrees

The use of bachelor's degrees as honorary degrees—never large —has declined in recent years.

The first honorary bachelor's degrees (see Chap. VI) were con-

17 Walter C. Eells, "Earliest Collegiate Degrees Authorized for Women," *Educational Horizons*, 39 (Summer, 1961), pp. 135–47.

18 Walter C. Eells, "Total Earned Degrees Conferred by Major American Institutions of Higher Education," *School and Society*, 89 (November 4, 1961), pp. 373–75.

ferred by Harvard College in 1692 upon its two tutors. John Leverett and William Brattle, both of whom had received their A.B. degrees from Harvard in 1680 and had been tutors since 1685, were awarded the honorary degree of Bachelor of Sacred Theology. This was evidently considered a greater distinction than the Bachelor of Arts, and therefore had the effect of bestowing greater prestige on the two tutors who, together with the president (who received an honorary doctorate at the same time), comprised the complete faculty of the young college.

Harvard conferred an honorary Bachelor of Arts degree in 1831 and Columbia conferred one in 1835. Princeton granted five honorary A.B. degrees in 1864. One student, who left Columbia in his junior year to enter the U. S. Military Academy at West Point, was graduated from the Academy in 1830. Columbia then gave him what was designated as an honorary A.B., although it would not be so considered now.[19] There are currently numerous cases in which a student studies at a liberal arts college for two or three years and then transfers to a university for professional work—engineering, for example—upon the completion of which he is awarded a degree from the first institution attended. This, however, is considered an earned degree, not an honorary one.

Epler reports that of the various honorary degrees conferred from 1872 to 1900, less than four percent were honorary bachelor's degrees. He says that an outstanding change after 1900 was the increase in honorary doctorates and the decline of honorary master's and bachelor's degrees.[20]

Thirteen different honorary baccalaureate degrees were reported in 1960 as having been in recent use. The only ones of these used by more than one institution, however, were the Bachelor of Arts, which had been used by 18 institutions and the Bachelor of Science, which had been used by 14.

---

[19] Stephen Edward Epler, *Honorary Degrees: A Survey of Their Use and Abuse* (Washington, D.C.: American Council on Public Affairs, 1943), p. 20.

[20] *Ibid.*, pp. 47, 73.

CHAPTER VIII

The Associate's Degree

Upon the recommendation of the Faculty of the Junior Colleges and of the Senate, and upon approval of the University Congregation, the Trustees have voted to confer the title or degree of Associate upon those students who finish the work of the Junior Colleges. . . . The proposed policy has already excited some interest. It is hoped that the new plan may receive the careful consideration of other institutions interested in the same problems.

William Rainey Harper, President, University of Chicago [1]

The associate's degree is the newest of the major American collegiate degrees, developing almost entirely after the beginning of the twentieth century. Although it has been considered typically a junior college degree, it is now awarded by many four-year colleges and universities as well and usually represents two years of work of college grade. It is estimated that approximately half a million associate's degrees of various types have been conferred in the United States since 1900.

Early History in Great Britain

Like the other established degrees, the associate's degree can be traced back to European origin. The Associate in Physical Science was authorized at the University of Durham, England, in 1865 to mark the completion of a two-year course of study in the newly established School of Physical Science. In practice, however, it appears to have been conferred first in 1873, when it was designated the Associate in Science (a form in current use in the United States). In 1877, Associate in Engineering and Associate in Coal Mining degrees were granted by Yorkshire College, which later became the University of Leeds. During this period, associate's degrees were also conferred by the University College of Wales and by the Royal College of Science, Dublin. In 1927, 13 types of asso-

---

[1] University of Chicago, *President's Report*, pp. xx–xxi.

ciate degrees, including the Associate in Theology and Associate in Music, were reported in use in British universities.[2]

Webster's *New International Dictionary* (2nd ed.) reports a unique British use of the Associate in Arts—it was conferred on men who passed the Oxford Senior Local Examination if they were *under 19 years of age*. This practice, however, was dropped several years ago.

Early History in the United States [3]

The University of Chicago, which opened in 1892 under the presidency of William Rainey Harper, was divided into four groups of colleges. Each of these was subdivided into an academic college, comprising the first two years, and a university college, comprising the last two years. These soon came to be known instead as the "junior college" and the "senior college." These divisions, and the degrees conferred at the conclusion of each course of study, are shown below:

Years	College of Liberal Arts	College of Literature	College of Science	College of Practical Arts
Freshman and Sophomore (Junior College)	Associate in Arts	Associate in Literature	Associate in Science	Associate in Science
Junior and Senior (Senior College)	Bachelor of Arts	Bachelor of Philosophy	Bachelor of Science	Bachelor of Science

Why the Senior College of the College of Literature should not have led to the Bachelor of Literature rather than the Bachelor of Philosophy is not clear. The College of Practical Arts was later designated the College of Commerce and Administration.

At first only certificates were granted for completion of the junior colleges, but on September 30, 1899, the board of trustees voted to

---

[2] For references to original sources for these statements, see Walter Crosby Eells, *Associate's Degree and Graduation Practices in Junior Colleges* (Washington, D.C.: American Association of Junior Colleges, 1942), pp. 6–8. See also J. M. Moore, "Associate of Arts Degree and Its European Counterpart: An Evaluation," *Junior College Journal*, 29 (April, 1959), pp. 469–73.

[3] Most of the information in this section is taken from Eells, *op. cit.*, pp. 8–14. which gives references to original sources.

adopt the associate's degree and 83 such degrees were conferred in the following academic year. Students who had earlier received a certificate were thereafter also called associates.

In 1932 the Carnegie Foundation erroneously reported that the Associate in Arts had been in use since 1891.[4] Nevertheless, inconvertible evidence shows that its first use in America was in 1900 at the University of Chicago, which was chartered in 1891, but did not open for instruction until 1892.

No direct evidence is available to show whether President Harper, and the various committees and groups which considered the matter for several years before 1900, were familiar with the English practice of conferring associate's degrees, but it is not unlikely that they were.

The action of the University had an immediate effect. Nicholas Murray Butler of Columbia University commented in an editorial in the influential *Educational Review:* "By establishing an academic designation to be conferred at the close of a two-year's college course, the University of Chicago has taken a step of national importance." [5] And in 1899 the U. S. Commissioner of Education commented favorably upon the action of the University of Chicago and quoted President Harper's statement of the benefits that he expected to follow from the use of the new degree: [6]

> It is believed that the results will be five-fold: (1) Many students will find it convenient to give up college work at the end of the sophomore year; (2) many students who would not otherwise do so will undertake at least two years of college work; (3) the professional schools will be able to raise their standards for admission and in any case many who desire a professional education will take the first two years of college work; (4) many academies and high schools will be encouraged to develop higher work; (5) many colleges which have not the means to do the work of the junior and senior years will be satisfied under this arrangement to do the lower work.

This prophetic statement has since been realized—perhaps even more fully than the author could have anticipated.

---

[4] Carnegie Foundation Commission, *State Higher Education in California* (Sacramento, Calif.: State Department of Education, 1932), p. 35. For full discussion of this statement, see Eells, *op. cit.,* p. 13.

[5] "A Two-Year College Course," *Educational Review,* 19 (April, 1900), p. 411.

[6] U. S. Commissioner of Education, *Annual Report,* 1898–99, p. 1562.

In 1918 the University of Chicago Board of Trustees, in connection with a departmental reorganization of the University, voted to discontinue the use of the associate's degree. But between 1899–1900 and 1919–20, a total of 4,462 such degrees had been granted, and their use had spread to institutions in all parts of the country, particularly in the newly developing independent junior colleges. The Associate in Arts, however, was reëstablished at the University of Chicago in 1931 and continued until 1942. High school graduates could qualify for it by passing seven "comprehensive examinations." [7]

The former Lewis Institute (which combined in 1940 with the Armour Institute to form the Illinois Institute of Technology) opened in 1896 as a junior college and in 1901 conferred the Associate in Literature or the Associate in Science on 22 graduates. In 1904 these degrees were replaced by the Associate in Arts, probably the first use of this degree by an independent junior college in the United States. This has become by far the most extensive associate's degree throughout the country. Even after it had become a four-year institution, the Institute continued to use the Associate in Arts and granted more than 1,000 before 1940, when it merged with the Armour Institute. The Associate in Domestic Economy, instituted in 1908, was granted to 650 women before 1932.

The influence of the University of Chicago can be seen in the case of California College, in Oakland, California (a small Baptist institution which closed about 1910). In its catalogue of February, 1900 it announced that "beginning with next August it will offer . . . two new courses of study, the one leading to the degree of Associate of Arts, the other to the Associate of Letters."

The first associate's degree to be conferred by any junior college still in existence in 1962 was probably awarded by Stephens College, Missouri, which became a junior college in 1911 and conferred the Associate in Arts on its first graduating class of eight young women in 1912. The first publicly controlled junior college to award such a degree was the Junior College of Kansas City, Missouri, which was organized in 1915 and conferred the Associate in Arts on its first graduating class of one young man and seven young women in 1916.

---

[7] University of Chicago, *Historical Statement of Curricular Requirements, 1931–1947* (Chicago, Ill.: nine-page mimeographed statement), p. 1.

Associate in Arts as a Four-Year Degree

The Associate in Arts has become exclusively a two-year degree. But for almost a quarter of a century it was offered by Harvard University and a group of eight associated Massachusetts institutions as the equivalent to a bachelor's degree upon completion of a four-year course of extension study. In 1910 the Overseers of Harvard University voted: [8]

> To confer the degree of Associate in Arts upon nonresident students who have attended the class exercises, completed the other work, and passed the examinations in the University Extension Courses (including summer courses) equal in number and standard to the courses required of a resident student for the degree of Bachelor of Arts.

In the next twenty years at least 129 such four-year Associate in Arts degrees were awarded, including 61 by Harvard University, 64 by Radcliffe College, and four by Tufts College.

This practice was abandoned by Harvard University in 1933 because of the increasing use of the Associate in Arts as a two-year college degree. President A. Lawrence Lowell, of Harvard, in his letter of May 10, 1933, to the President of the American Association of Junior Colleges, formally renounced all rights to the degree of Associate in Arts, but announced as a substitute for it as an extension degree the new degree of Adjunct in Arts, "claiming possession of it in fee simple." [9]

Use of Associate's Degree in Later Years

The first comprehensive study of junior colleges was made by McDowell in 1918 in a doctoral dissertation presented at the State University of Iowa. He found that of the 74 institutions then in existence from which he could secure data, 17, or 23 percent, were awarding the Associate in Arts degree.[10]

An extensive survey by the American Association of Junior Col-

[8] Harvard University, *Quinquennial Catalogue of Officers and Graduates, 1636–1930* (Cambridge, Mass.: Harvard University, 1930), p. 1129.

[9] W. C. Eells, *op. cit.,* p. 21.

[10] F. M. McDowell, *The Junior College* (Washington, D.C.: U.S. Department of the Interior: Bureau of Education, Bulletin 1919, No. 35), pp. 69, 124–27.

leges in 1941–42 reported that the associate's degree was offered by 244 junior colleges, or 40 percent of those then in existence.[11] In 1960, 444 junior colleges (including a few technical institutes and other two-year institutions not designated as junior colleges) out of 583 such institutions, or 75 percent, reported use of the associate's degree.[12]

In an incomplete study of the use of the associate's degree by four-year institutions, the American Association of Junior Colleges in 1942 identified 17 four-year colleges and universities which were then conferring this degree for courses of study less than four-years in length. In 1960 a complete report from all higher educational institutions in this country showed 156 four-year institutions (including 27 universities, 82 liberal arts colleges, 20 teachers colleges, and 27 other institutions) offering the associate's degree.[13]

Unfortunately the U.S. Office of Education does not include associate's degrees in its annual reports of number of degrees conferred by institutions in the United States. Such statistics for junior colleges, however, have been collected at four-year intervals since 1940 by the American Association of Junior Colleges and published in the successive editions of its reference volume, *American Junior Colleges*. The 1960 volume reports more than 44,000 associate degrees awarded in 1958–59. Statistics for accredited colleges and universities have been collected since 1956 by the American Council on Education, which published its findings in the 1956 and 1960 editions of *American Universities and Colleges*. The 1960 edition reports the awarding of almost 14,000 associate degrees. These make a total of over 58,000, by both types of institutions in 1958–59. It is probable that those awarded by nonaccredited institutions (not included in these volumes) would bring the total of such degrees awarded in 1958–59 close to 60,000. More than one-third of the degrees awarded by junior colleges were conferred by the 66 junior colleges in California.

The associate's degree serves two rather distinct functions. It gives suitable academic recognition to the completion of a "general"

11 W. C. Eells, *op. cit.*, p. 21.

12 Walter Crosby Eells and Harold A. Haswell, *Academic Degrees: Earned and Honorary Degrees Conferred by Institutions of Higher Education in the United States* (Washington, D.C.: U.S. Department of Health, Education, and Welfare: Office of Education, 1960), p. 21.

13 *Ibid.*, p. 21.

or liberal arts course prior to possible advanced specialization in a university. It thus represents the first significant rung on the collegiate ladder. In other cases it marks the conclusion of a specialized terminal, vocational, or semiprofessional curriculum, both in junior colleges and in some universities, for students who finish their formal collegiate education at the sophomore level. In either case the recipient enjoys the prestige and recognition and the sense of satisfaction and completeness that come from the possession of a college degree.

Varieties of Associate's Degrees

In 1960 no less than 137 varieties of associate's degrees were reported as conferred. Another 12 had been used in the past but were no longer in use. By far the most common of these is the Associate in Arts, reported in use by 529 institutions, both junior colleges and four-year institutions. It is the only associate's degree authorized for all of the junior colleges in California, which has more such institutions than any other State. It is one of the three authorized by the New York Board of Regents for use in that state. The next most popular is the Associate in Science (also authorized by the New York Board of Regents), which is offered by 122 institutions. Other associate degrees offered by twenty or more institutions are: Associate in Applied Science, 81 (authorized by New York Board of Regents); Associate in Business Administration, 37; Associate in Education, 32; Associate in Engineering, 32; Associate in Secretarial Science, 25; Associate in Commerce, 25; and Associate in Business, 24.

The American Association of Junior Colleges found that of the individuals who had received the various associate degrees from 1910 to 1941, 83 percent had received the Associate in Arts, nine percent the Associate in Science, and eight percent all other associate degrees.

A similar analysis (based upon the 1960 edition of *American Junior Colleges*) of the individuals who received the different associate degrees in 1959 showed a decrease in proportion of those receiving the Associate of Arts, an increase in proportion of those receiving the Associate in Science. The degrees received by more than one per cent of the total number were:

Degree	Institutions	Individuals	Percent of Total
Associate in Arts	404	32,940	72.9
Associate in Science	128	6,404	14.2
Associate in Applied Science	16	2,443	5.4
Associate in Business Administration	11	1,238	2.7
Associate in Engineering	20	893	2.0
33 Other Associate's degrees, each less than 1%	—		
		1,284	2.8
Total		45,202	100.0

CHAPTER IX

Other Degrees

A degree is a mere toy if I do not care for the work beneath it.
M. Carey Thomas, President of Bryn Mawr College,
while an undergraduate student at Cornell University [1]

The great majority of degrees used by American colleges and universities are comprised in the four major types—doctor's, master's, bachelor's, and associate's degrees. But there are several others which have passed or are passing from use, and at least one new group which promises to be more widely used in the future.

Occupational Designation Degrees

The most frequently found of the degrees other than those already considered is a group of some forty which are designations of different occupations or professions. These are found chiefly in the engineering fields. The one most frequently reported in 1960 was Mechanical Engineer (M.E.), offered by 13 institutions, followed by Civil Engineer (C.E.) by 11, Electrical Engineer (E.E.) by 11, Chemical Engineer (Ch.E.) by ten, Metallurgical Engineer (Met.E.) by nine, and Engineer of Mines (E.M.) by seven.

In addition, one or two institutions each give similar occupationally designated degrees in the fields of aeronautical, agricultural, architectural, ceramic, geodetic, geological, geophysical, industrial, marine, naval, nuclear, petroleum, and sanitary engineering. The simple "Engineer" is also found, as well as Professional Engineer, Professional Agricultural Engineer, and a half dozen other specialized "Professional" engineers.

Usually these are second level engineering degrees, awarded a year or more after a baccalaureate degree in engineering. In some cases these degrees require a definite course of advanced study; in

---

[1] Edith Finch, *Carey Thomas of Bryn Mawr* (New York: Harper & Brothers, 1947), p. 77.

others they represent several years of successful engineering practice and presentation of a thesis or other professional report. But requirements vary widely with different degrees, different institutions, and different periods. Occasionally they are awarded as honorary degrees.

Originally the more common of these were awarded as first degrees in engineering, the equivalent of the bachelor's degree. Thus the first engineering college, Rensselaer Polytechnic Institute (founded in 1824) was given the right by charter to confer the degrees of Civil Engineer and Topographical Engineer as well as Bachelor of Science (see p. 9). It awarded C.E. degrees for the first time to four young men in 1835. They were conferred with cautious reservations, however, as indicated by the following report to the president by a committee of three faculty members: [2]

> We have examined Edward Suffern, William Clement, Jacob Eddy, and Amos Westcott as candidates for the degree of Civil Engineer. We find them acquainted with the theory of practice. But as this is the first class proposed to be graduated, their own honor and the honor of this institution demand great caution in conferring degrees. We therefore recommend as follows: that they receive the degrees, but that the diplomas be left with the Secretary until the President shall receive satisfactory certificates that they have reviewed their Textbooks (outlines Gregory), that they can read algebraic equations, and have a general Knowledge of Perspective generally.

In the next 60 years, the Institute conferred 982 C.E. degrees, but only five of Topographical Engineer (all in a single year, 1860). C.E. degrees were also awarded by Dartmouth College in 1845, by the University of Michigan in 1855, and by Yale University in 1860. Columbia University awarded its first E.M. degree in 1867.

By the early twentieth century these degrees were coming to be used as graduate degrees. Thus a Committee of the Association of American Universities reported in 1916 that of 92 institutions studied, 62 applied the professional degrees of C.E., M.E., and so on, as graduate degrees, while only 16 used them as first degrees equivalent to baccalaureate degrees. The Committee recommended

---

[2] Palmer C. Ricketts, *History of Rensselaer Polytechnic Institute, 1824–1894* (New York: John Wiley and Sons, 1895), p. 80.

that these degrees be reserved to mark the completion study beyond the level of the master's degree.[3]

The report of the latest comprehensive survey of engineering education, published by the Society for the Promotion of Engineering Education (now the American Society for Engineering Education) in 1930, repeated the recommendations of a special committee of 1910: [4]

> A four-year engineering course should normally lead to the degree of Bachelor of Science (B.S.) to which should be added a specifying phrase, as for example Bachelor of Science in Civil Engineering (B.S. in C.E.).
> The professional engineering degrees, C.E., M.E., etc., should be given only to graduates who present satisfactory evidence of professional work of superior quality extending over not less than three years, and who submit a satisfactory thesis.

Current practice is in general accordance with these recommendations. In 1960 there were 33 institutions which offered the Bachelor of Civil Engineering (B.C.E.), 83 which offered the Bachelor of Science in Civil Engineering (B.S.C.E.); and 15 which offered the Master of Civil Engineering (M.C.E.), 33 which gave the Master of Science in Civil Engineering (M.S.C.E.), as contrasted with the 11 institutions offering the degree of C.E.,[5] and probably most of these represented work above the baccalaureate level.

At the Massachusetts Institute of Technology, according to its catalogue, these "Engineer" degrees represent "a more advanced level and a broader range of competence in engineering and science than that required for the master's degree, but with less emphasis on creative research than that characterizing a doctoral program." In general the master's degree represents one year and the "Engineer"

---

[3] Armin O. Leuschner, Chairman, "Report of Committee on Academic and Professional Degrees," Association of American Universities, *Proceedings,* 1916; report, pp. 65–77; discussion, pp. 92–9.

[4] Society for the Promotion of Engineering Education, *Report of the Investigation of Engineering Education, 1923–1929* (Pittsburgh, Pa.: The Society, 1930), 2 vols. Bulletin No. 7, "A Study of Engineering Degrees," pp. 356–67, a study of 150 institutions offering engineering curricula. See also "Report of the Committee on Engineering Degrees," in the Society's *Proceedings,* 1910, pp. 135–55.

[5] See Walter Crosby Eells and Harold A. Haswell, *Academic Degrees: Earned and Honorary Degrees Conferred by Institutions of Higher Education in the United States* (Washington, D.C.: U.S. Department of Health, Education, and Welfare: Office of Education, 1960), pp. 125–43.

degrees two years of work beyond the baccalaureate. Fourteen such engineering programs are listed, each requiring a thesis.

At the Missouri School of Mines a professional engineering degree "is considered an honorary degree" to be awarded after five years to a man "in a responsible position in the engineering profession."

Rensselaer Polytechnic Institute, the first to grant C.E. degrees, now confines itself to bachelor's, master's, and doctor's degrees in the various engineering fields.

Other occupationally designated degrees, in current use by only one or two institutions, include Dental Hygienist, Engineering Geologist, Forester, Naval Architect, Pharmaceutical Chemist, Professional Architect, and Wood Technologist.

Licentiate and Other Degrees

The degree of "Licentiate" is commonly used in France and Spain and in French- and Spanish-speaking universities in North and South America, usually as a first degree. In Great Britain it has represented a degree preliminary to the master's degree.

A score of different licentiate degrees were formerly offered in the United States, usually representing a level between the master's and doctor's degrees, but now are seldom awarded except by a few theological institutions which offer the Licentiate in Sacred Theology or Licentiate in Theology. In 1960 the Licentiate in Canon Law, Licentiate in Philosophy, and Licentiate in Dramatic Art were reported in use—each by one institution. Degrees of this type formerly given include licentiates in medicine, surgery, and pharmacy.

The degree of "Graduate" was formerly awarded in about a score of different fields. In 1960 it was reported offered in the fields of agriculture, architecture, dentistry, law, nursing, and social work —each by one institution.

A half dozen varieties of the degree of "Laureate" have been conferred, but none of these are currently used.

Harvard's special use of the degree of Adjunct in Arts has already been mentioned (see p. 98).

Degrees for Women

Special degrees for women—Mistress, Sister, and Maid—existed for almost a century until 1925 (see Chap. VII). In other efforts to avoid the connotation of "bachelor" some institutions in the nineteenth century conferred on women graduates the neutral degrees of "Graduate" or "Laureate." Thus Graduate in Letters, Laureate of English Literature, and Laureate of Science were early degrees conferred on women, but none of these are used today.

Specialist Degrees

Unlike the various special types of degrees which appear to be disappearing, a new degree in the professional field of education has developed since 1950 and appears to be growing more popular. It is intermediate between the master's and doctor's degrees, usually representing two years of work beyond the baccalaureate, and frequently designated as a "sixth-year degree." The name of this new degree is not yet firmly established, but in 1960 Specialist in Education was offered by ten institutions, while Education Specialist and Educational Specialist were offered by two institutions each, the abbreviation Ed.S. being used for all three. This level of work is also designated by the degrees Advanced Degree in Education (Ed.A.), Advanced Master of Education (A.M.E.), and Advanced Master of Arts in Education (A.M.A.E.).

This "Specialist" degree was first offered by the University of Kansas in 1950 and granted there in 1954.[6] Several other institutions, however, including Johns Hopkins, Boston, and Stanford, conferred six-year degrees in education under other titles as early as 1933 and 1934.[7] The AACTE, in its 1960 study, listed 59 institutions as granting some type of sixth-year degree in education, and 20 more which were planning to offer it before 1967.[8]

Suggestions for sixth-year degrees designed especially for college teachers in fields other than education include the Master of Philosophy (M.Ph. or M.Phil.) in all fields, analogous to the Ph.D., but without the requirement of a thesis and with specific pedagogical content and practice.[9]

---

[6] Robert H. Koenker, *Sixth-Year Graduate Programs in Teacher Education* (Muncie, Ind.: Ball State Teachers College, October 1957), 81 pp., mimeographed.

[7] Harold E. Moore, John H. Russel, and Donald G. Ferguson, *The Doctorate in Education: Vol. II, The Institutions* (Washington, D.C.: American Association of Colleges for Teacher Education, 1960), p. 90.

[8] *Ibid.*, p. 91–2.

[9] Everett Walters, "What Degree for College Teachers?" *Journal of Higher Education*, 31 (February, 1960), pp. 69–74; and "A New Degree for College Teachers," *Journal of Higher Education*, 31 (May, 1960), pp. 282–4.

CHAPTER X

Needed Improvements In Degrees

> At the present time no less than two hundred and thirty-eight degrees are conferred. Among the more trivial of new degrees—and most of them are trivial—are many which contain the Bachelorship as applied to specific arts—Bachelor of Accounts, B.Acct.; Bachelor of Business Science, B.B.S.; Bachelor of Elements, B.E.; Bachelor of Elementary Didactics, B.E.D.; Bachelor of Finance, B.F. . . ; Master of Domestic Economy, M.D.E.; and many others equally, or, if possible, more unworthy of having a place with great historic symbols.
>
> President Charles F. Thwing, Western Reserve University, 1906 [1]

The need for standardizing the nomenclature of degrees and reducing the number of different degrees offered by American universities and colleges is much greater than it was almost half a century ago when their number and triviality were deplored by President Thwing.

In this final chapter, a few suggestions will be made for needed improvements with reference to college degrees and the abbreviations commonly used for them and more adequate reporting of "degree" information. No attempt will be made, however, to consider the broader and more controversial problem of the content of the various courses leading to the different degrees, nor the problem of the relative emphasis on teaching and research in preparation for graduate degrees. These are subjects which will continue to engage the attention of various educational organizations, especially the Council of American Graduate Schools organized at Chicago in March 1961. Possible modifications in function and content of the master's and doctor's degrees have been discussed by a special committee of the Association of Graduate Schools, as well as by other organizations in earlier years.[2] But these problems are a matter of

---

[1] Charles F. Thwing, *History of Higher Education in America* (New York: D. Appleton and Company, 1906), p. 429.

[2] See Association of Graduate Schools in the Association of American Universities, *Proceedings,* 1955, pp. 11–47; 1956, pp. 8–81, 106–24; 1957, 33–48; and 1958, pp. 31–49.

curricula, not of degrees as such, and so are beyond the scope of this volume.

Number of Different Degrees

In 1960 the colleges and universities of the country reported that they were offering more than 1,600 different degrees. Although the twentieth century has witnessed the marked development and differentiation of schools, curricula, and fields of specialization, yet the number of degrees now offered is far in excess of all legitimate requirements. Many of them differ only in minor terminology, such as Bachelor of Civil Engineering, Bachelor of Arts in Civil Engineering, Bachelor of Science in Civil Engineering, or Bachelor of Science in Engineering in Civil Engineering. Others are unnecessarily detailed and cumbersome, as Bachelor of Music in Trumpet, Master of Arts in Teaching College Humanities, or Bachelor of Science in Engineering in Naval Architecture and Marine Engineering. What is the essential difference between the Bachelor of Science in Education, given by 264 institutions, the Bachelor of Arts in Education, given by 55, and the simple Bachelor of Education, given by 52? [3]

Usually such minor variations in terminology may be attributed, at least in part, to lack of knowledge of what other institutions are doing. This is not always the case, however. For example, the University of North Carolina confers both the Master of Public Health and the Master of Science in Public Health. If there is an essential difference in the two degrees, it probably will be seldom recognized away from the Chapel Hill campus.

Complete standardization is neither necessary nor desirable. Freedom for experimentation in various fields is characteristic of higher education in the United States, and should be continued and encouraged. But with reference to the use of academic degrees, liberty has become license. Of the 1,600 different degrees mentioned above, more than 1,000 are conferred by only one institution in the case of each type.

---

[3] Most of the information in this and the following section are taken from Walter Crosby Eells and Harold A. Haswell, *Academic Degrees: Earned and Honorary Degrees Conferred by Institutions of Higher Education in the United States* (Washington, D.C.: U.S. Department of Health, Education, and Welfare: Office of Education, 1960), Chaps. VII and VIII, pp. 59–201, which contain much related information.

It is highly questionable, too, whether different degrees are needed to indicate *method* as well as *content*. Why should Harvard University require the degree of Adjunct in Arts (see p. 98) to represent the work for the standard Bachelor of Arts degree when it happens to have been done in extension courses? Why should the University of Oklahoma have established in 1961 the new degree of Bachelor of Liberal Studies (with a special foundation grant of $61,000 to finance pilot groups) to indicate the completion of a liberal arts course by adult, part-time students? [4] If the work of students in these courses at Harvard or Oklahoma represents the equivalent of the A.B. degree, why should they not receive that degree, regardless of their age or place and method of study? Or is the establishment of such degrees implicit admission on the part of the university authorities that they are not really the equivalent of the degrees won by adolescent full-time students? What is the line between an adolescent and an adult? Why should they receive different degrees?

Abbreviations for Degrees

A reduction in the number of abbreviations used for degrees is also badly needed. Almost 2,600 abbreviations are found for the 1,600 different degrees mentioned above, involving unnecessary duplication and confusion even in academic circles, and much more so on the part of the general public. For about a thousand of these degrees, two or more abbreviations are used; in about a hundred cases there are as many as five different abbreviations; and in 14 cases ten or more abbreviations for a single degree are found. For the degree of Bachelor of Science in Chemical Engineering, for example, the following 14 abbreviations are reported as used by different institutions: B.S.Ch.E., B.S. (Ch.E.), B.S.Ch.Eng., B.S. Chem.E., B.S. in C.E., B.S. in Ch.E., B.S. in Ch.Eng., B.S. in Ch.Engin., B.S. in Chm.E., B.S. in Chem.E., B.S. in Chem.Eng., B.S. in Chem.Engi., B.S. in Chem.Engr., and B.S. in Chem.

Such a multiplicity of abbreviations is far in excess of any possible legitimate needs. The first one, B.S.Ch.E., would meet all needs and would promote simplicity and uniformity. There should be little confusion in using "E" for both Engineering and Education. Engi-

---

[4] J. Clayton Feaver, "Bachelor of Liberal Studies Degree," *Adult Education*, 11 (Winter, 1961), pp. 110–17.

neering has priority rights on "E" from more than a century's use (C.E. has been in use since 1835), while Education can and should be standardized as "Ed.," as in Ed.D., M.Ed., and B.Ed., and various other degrees in education.

Seven other degrees have more than ten abbreviations each: Bachelor of Science in Business Administration, Bachelor of Science in Education, Bachelor of Science in Home Economics, Bachelor of Science in Nursing, Bachelor of Science in Pharmacy, Master of Science in Education, and Doctor of Letters.

On the other hand, in more than 200 cases, a single abbreviation is used which may stand for two or more different degrees. Thus "M.E." has been used to indicate Master of Education, Master of Elements, Master of Engineering, Mechanical Engineer, Military Engineer, Mining Engineer, or Mistress of English.

Even the order of letters in an abbreviation shows surprising variations. Thus B.A. is used by more than 500 institutions while more than 400 use the reverse order A.B. for the classic Bachelor of Arts. There is not even uniformity in this respect in the same institution: at least a score of institutions report the use of both forms for this degree. One uses B.A. in the college catalog, but A.B. in its permanent records. At the master's level, some 250 institutions use M.A. for Master of Arts, while 40 use A.M. At the Doctor's level, 20 use D.Ed., while 69 use Ed.D. Many other similar examples could be given. Standardization of abbreviations for the same degree should not be difficult to achieve. While not the most essential reform, it would certainly tend to improve the present situation, since most degrees, when used in connection with the name of an individual, are usually indicated by abbreviation only.

When new degrees are established too, care should be taken to see that they do not duplicate titles or abbreviations already established. For example the abbreviation announced for the University of Oklahoma's newly established Bachelor of Liberal Studies is, logically, B.L.S. But this is already the recognized abbreviation for the older Bachelor of Library Science. A more appropriate abbreviation would be B.Lib.St. or B.Lib.Stud.

Reporting Degrees Conferred

Since the organization of the U.S. Office of Education (as a Department in 1867; as a Bureau, 1867–1929) its chief purpose, as defined in the organic Act creating it, has been to provide a center of educational influence in the country with special emphasis on the collection and diffusion of statistics and facts relative to education in all of its phases. As one important phase of its fulfillment of this mandate, the Office, ever since its organization almost a century ago, has collected and published annually or biennially (1918–46) more or less detailed statistics concerning the number and type of degrees conferred by the different higher educational institutions of the country.

Since 1948, these reports have appeared as separate monographs. The report for 1958–59, entitled *Earned Degrees Conferred: Bachelor's and Higher Degrees,* is a substantial volume of 198 pages. It gives the number of doctor's, master's and second level professional, and bachelor's and first level professional degrees awarded to men, to women, by each institution, and in each of 160 different fields of study. Beginning in 1961, the Office further refined this presentation by reporting separately the data for bachelor's degrees and for first professional degrees. This mass of detailed information is sufficient to satisfy almost any legitimate need for data on degrees at the baccalaureate and higher levels.

The greatest lack, however, in these otherwise comprehensive annual reports, is their failure to include data on associate's degrees conferred each year. Approximately 60,000 associate's degrees are conferred annually in the United States (see Chap. VIII), not only by junior colleges but by numerous four-year institutions as well. This is six times as many as the number of doctor's degrees and almost as many as the number of master's degrees which are conferred each year. The number of associate's degrees is sure to increase further in future years. Yet the important facts concerning the number, type, and distribution of these recognized degrees, in spite of the legal mandate of the U. S. Office of Education for the "collection and diffusion of statistics and facts relative to education in *all* of its phases" are completely ignored by that agency.

This is a situation which should be corrected as soon as possible. Appropriate pressure, if necessary, should be brought to bear on the Department of Health, Education, and Welfare and on its Office of Education, by national educational organizations and other interested agencies.

Less essential, but also desirable, would be the collection of data regarding the number of honorary degrees granted each year. This was a service rendered by the Office of Education for seventy years, but abandoned in 1944. Information concerning the extent and growth, if any, of this practice would be useful in preventing or reducing abuse in this significant phase of American higher education.

Spurious Degrees

Legislation, especially at the state level, is badly needed to protect the public, not only in the United States but especially in foreign countries, against the so-called "degree mills," which, for a price, offer worthless degrees (see Chap. I).

Some progress has been made in the control of this evil, in some of the more flagrant cases, through Federal agencies, including the Department of State, Post Office Department, and Federal Trade Commission. But much remains to be done. Additional control is needed through the adoption by the various states of legislation to regulate the organization and activities of colleges so that only legitimate ones can be chartered and permitted to operate. In only a minority of the states is such regulatory legislation now found. A suggested model bill was proposed by the Committee on Fraudulent Schools and Colleges of the National Education Association in 1953, and given further publicity by the American Council on Education in 1959.[5] The college organizations found in a majority of the states that they could advantageously join with the Council of State Governments and various state agencies in promoting such legislation.

In 1959 the American Council on Education, through its Committee on Education and International Affairs, took a strong position to control this century-old evil, but the assistance and continued vigilance of national and state agencies, both public and private, are needed to maintain the purity and integrity of American college degrees in the face of the continued operation of disreputable degree mills.[6]

---

[5] Robert H. Reid, *American Degree Mills: A Study of Their Operations and of Existing and Potential Ways to Control Them* (Washington, D.C.: American Council on Education, 1959), pp. 79–83.

[6] The whole subject is discussed in Robert H. Reid, *op. cit.,* which contains a bibliography of 23 titles (pp. 98–99). See also Ronald Schiller, "Diploma Mills: America's Educational Underworld," *Reader's Digest* (June, 1960), pp. 53–7; and Eells and Haswell, *op. cit.,* pp. 53–8.

Agencies for Improvement

Certain general national organizations, such as the American Council on Education, the Association of American Universities, its affiliated Association of Graduate Schools, the more recently organized (1961) Council of American Graduate Schools, the Association of American Colleges, or the American Association of Junior Colleges, could well take the initiative in making recommendations for desirable reforms in collegiate degrees. The Association of American Universities for a few years had a Committee on Higher Academic and Professional Degrees which in 1924 made a number of recommendations regarding degrees in dentistry which have been followed to a considerable extent by dental schools. More such committees are needed.

Such committees might be particularly effective in limited specialized fields. Reduction and standardization of degrees are especially needed in the fields of engineering, education, business, and medical science, each of which reported the use of more than one hundred degrees in their particular fields in 1960. The engineering field led with 348 degrees—surely an excessive number. The American Society for Engineering Education would be the appropriate organization to undertake a study of reforms in its field, much as its Committees on Degrees did in 1910 and 1930.

From 50 to 90 degrees each were reported in 1960 in the following fields: agriculture, art, fine arts, law, music, public administration, and theology. Degree standardization might well engage the attention of appropriate national organizations in these fields. The U.S. Office of Education has suggested such activity to the officers of several of the organizations mentioned above.

In April 1962 the American Council on Education announced the appointment of an eight-member Committee on Academic Degrees, under the chairmanship of Dean W. G. Whaley of the Graduate School of the University of Texas. The announcement said that "the committee will prepare recommendations to limit the number of accepted academic degrees and to standardize the abbreviations."

Bibliography

Atkinson, Carroll, *Pro and Con of the Ph.D.* Boston, Mass.: Meador Publishing Co., 1945. Consists chiefly of extensive reprints of numerous articles on various phases of the Ph.D. 172 pp.

Blessing, James H., *Graduate Education: An Annotated Bibliography*, Bulletin 1961, No. 26. Washington, D.C.: U.S. Department of Health, Education, and Welfare: Office of Education, 1961. Contains 982 annotated references, chiefly of publications appearing in 1957–60, dealing with all phases of graduate education, many of them with master's and doctor's degrees. 151 pp.

Carmichael, Oliver C., *Graduate Education: A Critique and a Program.* New York: Harper & Brothers, 1961. Proposes two types of Doctor of Philosophy degrees: Phil.D. for those planning on college teaching; Ph.D. for those planning on other occupations. Also a three-year master's degree, coordinated with junior and senior years, Master of Philosophy (M.Phil.). 215 pp.

Chase, John L., *Doctoral Study: Fellowships and Capacity of Graduate Schools,* Circular No. 646, OE-54016. Washington, D.C.: U.S. Department of Health, Education, and Welfare: Office of Education, 1961. Based on reports from 139 doctorate-granting institutions. Shows existing institutions can accommodate a substantial number of additional doctoral candidates. More than 4,000 candidates have completed all requirements except their dissertations. 65 pp.

Commissioner of Education, *Annual Reports, 1872–1916. Biennial Survey of Education in the United States, 1916–18 to 1945–46. Earned Degrees Conferred: Bachelor's and Higher Degrees, 1947–48 to 1959–60.* These three series, published by the United States Office of Education, Washington, D.C., give an invaluable historical summary of degrees granted and various information concerning them covering almost a century of American higher education.

Eells, Walter Crosby, *Associate's Degree and Graduation Practices in Junior Colleges.* Washington, D.C.: American Association of Junior Colleges, 1942. Based chiefly on reports from 225 junior colleges. 126 pp.

Eells, Walter Crosby, and Harold A. Haswell, *Academic Degrees: Earned and Honorary Degrees Conferred by Institutions of Higher Education in the United States.* Washington, D.C.: U.S. Department of Health, Education, and Welfare: Office of Education, 1960. Primarily a catalogue of 1,600 degrees and their abbreviations offered by higher educational institutions in 1960, and of 800 degrees no longer conferred. 324 pp.

Epler, Stephen Edward, *Honorary Degrees: A Survey of Their Use and Abuse.* Washington, D.C.: American Council on Public Affairs, 1943. Based principally on study of seven institutions: Harvard, Yale, Smith, and Universities of California, Nebraska, North Carolina, and Wisconsin. 224 pp.

Foster, J. F., ed., *Commonwealth Universities Yearbook, 1960: A Directory of the Universities of the British Commonwealth and the Handbook of Their Association,* 38th ed. London: Association of Universities of the British Commonwealth, 1961. Gives full information on degrees awarded by 137 institutions. 1590 pp.

Gleazer, Edmund J., Jr., ed., *American Junior Colleges,* 5th ed. Washington, D.C.: American Council on Education. Gives information on associate's degrees conferred by 576 junior colleges in 1958–59. 564 pp.

Hollis, Ernest V., *Toward Improving Ph.D. Programs: Prepared for the Commission on Teacher Education.* Washington, D.C.: American Council on Education, 1945. A comprehensive discussion, including various analyses of 22,500 holders of the Ph.D. degree, 1930–40. 204 pp.

Irwin, Mary, ed., *American Universities and Colleges,* 8th ed. Washington, D.C.: American Council on Education, 1960. Gives information on degrees conferred and degree requirements for 1,058 four-year, regionally accredited institutions. Also summary of master's and doctor's degrees, 1861–1958. 1212 pp.

John, Walton C., *Graduate Study in Universities and Colleges in the United States,* Bulletin 1934, No. 20. Washington, D.C.: U.S. Department of the Interior: Office of Education, 1935. Gives extensive information on degrees and degree requirements a quarter of a century ago. 234 pp.

Ness, Frederic W., ed., *A Guide to Graduate Study: Programs Leading to the Ph.D. Degree,* 2nd ed. Washington, D.C.: American Council on Education, 1960. A comprehensive directory of programs, classified by fields of study, for 174 colleges and universities and briefer information concerning other doctoral degrees offered. 457 pp.

Reid, Robert H., *American Degree Mills: A Study of Their Operations and of Existing and Potential Ways to Control Them.* Washington, D.C.: American Council on Education, 1959. 99 pp.

Index

INSTITUTIONS AND ORGANIZATIONS ONLY

A

American Association for the Advancement of Science, 65, 66, 67
American Association of Colleges for Teacher Education, 28, 31, 32, 34, 106
American Association of Junior Colleges, v, 94, 98, 99, 100, 113
American Association of University Professors, 80
American Council on Education, 10, 39, 89, 99, 112, 113
American Medical Association, 62
American Philological Assocation, 65, 66, 67
American Society for Engineering Education, 104, 113
American Society of Dental Surgeons, 50
American Veterinary College, 51
American Women's College of Berlin, 41
Amherst College, 14, 66
Armour Institute, 97
Association of American Colleges, 113
Association of American Universities, 50, 69, 80, 103, 113
Association of Graduate Schools, 80, 107, 113
Association of Research Libraries, 36

B

Baltimore College of Dental Surgery, 50
Beaver College, 91
Boston University, 24, 41, 106
Bowdoin College, 14
British Privy Council, 55, 59
British universities, 3, 4, 9, 13, 53, 59, 62, 94, 95
Brown University, 59, 60, 68, 70, 80, 85
Bryn Mawr College, 40, 102
Bucknell University, 64

Burritt College, 91

C

California College, 97
Canadian universities, 7
Carnegie Foundation, 96
Carnegie Institute of Technology, 9, 10
Central High School, Philadelphia, 68, 89
Clark University, 26, 27, 29
College and Academy of Philadelphia (*see* University of Pennsylvania)
College of Cambridge (Harvard), 82
College of Charleston, 85
College of New Jersey (*see* Princeton University)
College of Rhode Island (*see* Brown University)
College of William and Mary, 4, 59, 62, 81, 85, 86
Columbia University, 11, 24, 26, 29, 34, 36, 47, 49, 53, 54, 58, 59, 65, 77, 84, 85, 88, 92, 93, 96, 103
Connecticut State Medical Society, 49
Cornell University, 24, 33, 38, 40, 41, 42, 51, 69, 102
Council of American Graduate Schools, 107, 112
Council of State Governments, 112
Cumberland University, 69

D

Dartmouth College, 9, 11, 26, 54, 55, 58, 59, 66, 68, 77, 84, 85, 103
Degrees (*see* Contents, pp. vii-viii)
DePauw University, 66
Dickinson College, 66, 85
Dillard University, 43

E

European universities, 3, 11, 13, 17, 21, 51, 72, 83, 86, 105
Ewing College, 69

F

Federation of Graduate Clubs, 67, 68, 69, 70
Florida State University, 33

G

Georgetown University, 62
Georgia Female College (*see* Wesleyan College)
German universities, 3, 4, 18, 20, 25
Gonzaga University, 65
Grove City College, 69

H

Hamilton College, 66
Hampden-Sydney College, 85
Harvard University (Harvard College), 4, 5, 11, 12, 13, 14, 24, 26, 27, 28, 29, 30, 31, 37, 39, 42, 44, 47, 50, 53, 54, 55, 56, 59, 60, 61, 62, 65, 66, 72, 73, 74, 76, 77, 81, 82, 83, 84, 85, 86, 93, 98, 109
Hunter College, 92

I

Illinois Institute of Technology, 97
Indiana University, 29
Italian universities, 12

J

Johns Hopkins University, 24, 25, 26, 27, 29, 39, 88, 106
Junior College of Kansas City, 97

K

Kansas City University, 69
King's College (*see* Columbia University)

L

Lafayette College, 66
Lawrence Scientific School, 86
Lewis Institute, 97
Lexington State Normal School, 29
Liberty Hall Academy (*see* Washington and Lee University)
London School of Medicine for Women, 50

M

Madison College, 66
Magdalen College, 14
Marietta College, 66
Massachusetts Institute of Technology, 38, 69, 104
Medical Institution of Geneva, 49
Missouri School of Mines, 105
Mount Holyoke College, 71

N

Nashville University, 66
National Education Association, 32, 66, 79, 112
National Society of College Teachers of Education, 34
New Orleans University, 43
New Windsor College, 69
New York College of Veterinary Surgeons, 51
New York Infirmary and College for Women, 50
New York State Department of Education, 10
New York University, 24, 25, 29, 42
Northwestern University, 9, 10, 29

O

Oberlin College, 9, 90
Ohio State University, 24, 26

P

Pennsylvania State University, 29
Phi Beta Kappa, 43
Philadelphia College of Pharmacy and Science, 52
Princeton University, 9, 11, 26, 38, 41, 47, 54, 59, 64, 66, 75, 77, 85, 93
Providence College, 65

Q

Queen's College (*see* Rutgers University)

R

Radcliffe College, 42, 44, 98
Rensselaer Polytechnic Institute, 9, 10, 69, 86, 103, 105
Royal College of Physicians, 58
Royal College of Science, 94
Russell Sage College, 70

Rutgers University, 29, 47, 59, 68, 84, 85

S

St. John's College, 85
St. Mary's University, 62
Scottish universities, 57
Sheffield Scientific School, 21
Smith College, 9, 42, 53, 70
Society for the Promotion of Engineering Education, 104
South American universities, 105
Spanish universities, 12
Spring Hill College, 69
Stanford University, 29, 106
Stephens College, 97
Stevens Institute of Technology, 9, 24, 26
Straight University, 43
Swarthmore College, 41
Swiss universities, 40
Syracuse University, 24, 41, 49, 68

T

Temple University, 29
Trinity College, Dublin, 56
Tufts College, 68, 71, 98

U

U.S. Military Academy, 8, 93
U.S. Naval Academy, 8
U.S. Office of Education, vi, 6, 10, 14, 35, 36, 37, 38, 39, 45, 48, 51, 64, 65, 77, 78, 79, 85, 87, 92, 99, 104, 108, 110, 111, 112, 113, 115
Union College and University, 59, 66, 68, 85
University College of Wales, 94
University of Bologna, 2, 16, 17, 18, 39, 40
University of California, 9, 10, 29, 53, 92
University of Cambridge, 3, 4, 12, 14, 18, 41, 55, 56, 57
University of Chicago, 27, 31, 44, 88, 89, 94, 95, 96, 97
University of Connecticut, 33
University of Durham, 94
University of Edinburgh, 57
University of Georgia, 33, 77
University of Göttingen, 21, 40
University of Illinois, 9, 33
University of Kansas, 106
University of Leeds, 94

University of Leipzig, 40
University of Maryland, 48, 50
University of Michigan, 24, 26, 33, 66, 76, 77, 78, 103
University of Minnesota, 9
University of Nebraska, 53
University of North Carolina, 53, 66, 77, 85, 108
University of North Dakota, 29
University of Notre Dame, 9
University of Oklahoma, 29, 109, 110
University of Oxford, 3, 4, 12, 14, 18, 55, 56, 57, 59, 82, 95
University of Padua, 40
University of Paris, 2, 17, 83
University of Pennsylvania, 24, 25, 39, 41, 44, 46, 47, 59, 60, 77, 84, 85, 86
University of Pittsburgh, 44
University of St. Andrews, 59, 82
University of Southern California, 29
University of Texas, 29, 31, 34, 113
University of the City of New York, 66
University of the State of New York, 10, 59, 62, 71
University of Virginia, 76
University of Wisconsin, 53, 66, 69
University of Zurich, 41

V

Vanderbilt University, 24, 80
Van Doren's College for Young Ladies, 91

W

Washington and Lee University, 85
Washington College (Maryland), 59, 60, 85
Washington College (Tennessee), 85
Wellesley College, 71
Wesleyan College, 89, 90
Wesleyan University, 13
Western Reserve University, 50, 66
Wheaton College (Illinois), 90
Williams College, 85

Y

Yale University (Yale College), 4, 5, 11, 12, 13, 21, 22, 23, 24, 27, 39, 42, 43, 49, 52, 54, 57, 58, 59, 60, 64, 69, 75, 76, 77, 80, 81, 82, 85, 103
Yorkshire College (*see* University of Leeds)